Rituals and Traditions

Rituals and Traditions

Fostering a Sense of Community in Preschool

Jacky Howell and Kimberly Reinhard

National Association for the Education of Young Children

National Association for the
Education of Young Children
1313 L Street NW, Suite 500
Washington, DC 20005-4101
202-232-8777 • 800-424-2460
www.naeyc.org

NAEYC Books

Chief Publishing Officer
Derry Koralek

Editor-in-Chief
Kathy Charner

Senior Creative Design Manager
Audra Meckstroth

Managing Editor
Mary Jaffe

Senior Editor
Holly Bohart

Senior Graphic Designer
Malini Dominey

Editorial Assistant
Ryan Smith

Through its publications
program, the National
Association for the Education
of Young Children (NAEYC)
provides a forum for discussion
of major issues and ideas in the
early childhood field, with the
hope of provoking thought and
promoting professional growth.
The views expressed or implied
in this book are not necessarily
those of the Association or its
members.

Photographs: Copyright © Julia Luckenbill: 10; Lynn A.
Manfredi/Petitt: 41; Karen Phillips: 21; Ellen Senisi: 29, 73;
Susan Woog Wagner (NAEYC Copyright): 79, 85

Courtesy of Beth Ann Moore: 2, 3, 8, 27, 44, 46, 63 (bottom),
77, 90

Courtesy of the Authors: 4, 6, 11, 13, 22, 24, 25, 32, 33 (top and
bottom), 34, 35, 43, 49, 52, 58, 63 (top), 70, 75, 88, 96 (all),
111 (top and bottom)

Credits

Cover design: Malini Dominey

Copy editor: Liz Wegner

Library of Congress Control Number: 2015941530

ISBN 978-1-938113-16-1

Item 183

Contents

Foreword

"If it hasn't been in the Hand, the Body and the Heart . . .
it cannot be in the Brain."

This phrase is the result of our effort to describe in as few words as possible our philosophy of how children learn. This tenet of ours has evolved over many years of working with young children and their families and from reading considerable research on early childhood education. Indeed, there are a number of resources for parents and educators about children, hands-on experiences, and learning in general, but not so much about how the heart must also be involved. As we read *Rituals and Traditions: Fostering a Sense of Community in Preschool*, it was soon apparent that this book is about the heart. The authors' thorough account of the importance of rituals and traditions and how they promote secure and safe environments where children learn and grow is a reminder that the heart is every bit as crucial as the hand and body.

Whenever we have a friend over for dinner, we ask for two things they are thankful for. We join hands around the table and sing their response: "We give thanks for food and friends," (then raise our hands overhead for) "Alleluia. We give thanks for food and friends, Alleluia." There was a period when our teenage daughters found this tradition most embarrassing, especially when the guest was a friend of theirs. Once, after a singing of grace, a daughter whispered to her friend, "Get used to it, it's what they do here." Yes, it is and with good reason. As authors Jacky Howell and Kimberly Reinhard remind us, rituals and traditions "assist children in times of stress, unite and connect people, create memories that last into adulthood, strengthen the bonds of a school, and build a strong community." Even when children resist certain traditions, as our daughters did, that awkward period will soon pass, and they will be the ones insisting we hang on to tradition.

The authors' support for and understanding of the tremendous value of ritual and tradition in the classroom comes from the best of sources—their very own personal experiences in the classroom and many years mentoring educators. This book is a continuation of their passion for teaching others, especially when they answer their question "Why Develop Rituals and Traditions?" What follows is everything an educator could want or need for making rituals and traditions an essential part of their own classroom practices. The authors present evidence for how rituals and traditions affect the lives of young children and their families and follow up with the nuts and bolts for how to make them happen.

"When teachers and directors in a program work with families to intentionally create rituals and traditions that families and children depend on, relate to, and connect with, they create a strong community that is united through shared rituals and traditions." The authors provide guidance for how to move beyond efforts like hanging a sign in a multipurpose room proclaiming "We Are All Friends Here!" or wearing T-shirts emblazoned with "I Love All Children" to creating rituals and traditions that support children's learning and development and improve the school community.

We encourage educators to read this book, share its message with others, and work toward making rituals and traditions a centerpiece of the time you spend with the young children in your care.

—Michael Leeman, Teacher, Co-Director, Roseville Community Preschool,
With Bev Bos, Author, Lecturer, Teacher, Co-Director,
Roseville Community Preschool

Introduction

Historically, rituals and traditions have been important to every culture. They can be the glue that connects families every day and helps them through challenging times. Although the research to support this statement is clear, there is not nearly as much research about the benefits of the rituals and traditions in a school community. Anecdotally, the evidence is clear. While writing her master's thesis, Jacky Howell heard from many children she taught and their families. They shared their memories, including many about the rituals and traditions that were part of the class and program where Jacky was a teacher. The impact and importance of these rituals far outlasted the time the children and families spent in Jacky's class. As you will read in this book, many families have continued these rituals and traditions. It is clear from the existing research and anecdotal information that this topic is critical to the field of early childhood education.

We have worked extensively with children in preschool classrooms, and we have discovered how rituals can assist children in stressful times, unite and connect people, create memories that last into adulthood, strengthen the bonds of a school, and build a strong community. We pulled together information from personal experiences, working with other teachers and programs, and the research on rituals and traditions so we could share how both can be used in early childhood settings. Many of the stories in this book come from our experiences as a teacher, director, and trainer.

The impact of creating rituals and traditions is long-lasting. They build connections and provide an opportunity for everyone—children, families, and staff—to learn about themselves and others. They create a safe, warm, and secure environment where children are able to learn and grow. They offer learning experiences for children, staff, and families alike. They positively enhance both program and classroom environments. Rituals can become traditions that may last long after children have left your classroom or you stop

teaching. This book provides information, anecdotes, and how to's so you can create rituals and traditions in your own classroom or preschool program.

We hope this book will encourage you to examine the rituals and traditions you have created or inspire you to begin developing rituals and traditions. We would love to hear about the rituals and traditions you develop. Write to us at ritualsandtraditions@gmail.com.

About This Book

Chapter 1 explains why rituals and traditions are important in a school community and classroom.

Chapter 2 describes daily rituals that can be used in the classroom.

Chapter 3 provides examples of weekly and monthly rituals, including how you can expand on daily rituals and how you can share the rituals with children, their families, and your colleagues.

Chapter 4 shares the importance of annual and seasonal traditions, including rituals such as incubating and hatching ducks and hosting Alumni Readathons to build a strong community.

Chapter 5 provides inspiration and information to create your own rituals and traditions, including a chart that outlines how to start building rituals and traditions into your daily, weekly, monthly, and yearly plans. What are the questions you need to ask? How do you start?

We hope you enjoy this book and that you share our belief that rituals and traditions can build a strong school community and create an environment that supports children's learning and development. We believe that if you start creating rituals and traditions, everyone—including you, the children, families, and your colleagues—will build long-lasting connections that contribute to a positive learning environment for all.

1
Creating Community With Rituals and Traditions

"How many cookies are we going to make for the I Love You Dinner?" Liza asks Jacky, her preschool teacher. "I think maybe 250." "Whoa—that will take a lot of days to cook!" says Liza. Jacky and the children start to make a big bowl of cookie batter. Liza and Kevin use big spoons to stir the ingredients. They use their whole body to push the chocolate chips into the batter. Suddenly, Liza stops stirring, and Jacky says, "We're almost done; just use a little more of your muscles." "No, Jacky, stop!" Liza insists. "My Band Aid is in there!" Liza points to the big bowl of dough. Jacky sighs and smiles, thinking that this will be another memory for the I Love You Dinner tradition file!

The Power of Traditions

For more than 15 years, the I Love You Dinner was a tradition in Jacky's preschool class. The children created invitations, walked to the post office to mail them, counted the days until the mail reached their homes, and shopped at the grocery store to buy the food. For the next four days, the children, teachers, and families prepared food by making homemade spaghetti sauce, baking hundreds of chocolate chip cookies, tossing a salad, and buttering *a lot* of bread. Meanwhile, the teachers and children selected two or three songs to sing with their families on the big night. One song that the children chose for the first I Love You Dinner, and every other dinner was the traditional folk song "Skinnamarink," with its most important line—"I love you!"

Many years later, a former preschooler invited Jacky over for dinner when the student was home from college. To Jacky's surprise and delight, the menu consisted of spaghetti with tomato sauce, salad, bread with butter, and chocolate chip cookies! Clearly, the I Love You Dinner tradition became their family's tradition.

In early childhood programs, sharing meals with children is part of the daily routine. In Jacky's classroom, the I Love You Dinner became an annual tradition with its own unique rituals, including the menu and the favorite songs the children sang each year. It was created with the intention of building a community of teachers, families, and children. Over time, it became a beloved tradition in Jacky's center.

Rituals and traditions are part of everyday life. A ritual can be reading a book in a special chair before bed. A tradition can be a special food that is served only at celebrations. Rituals and traditions have the power to shape classroom routines into times that build meaningful connections and bonds among children, families, and teachers, creating and strengthening a sense of community in early childhood settings.

What Are Routines, Rituals, and Traditions?

What are rituals and traditions, and how do they differ from routines? Routines are repeated, predictable events that are planned parts of the day, week, or month. According to Gillespie and Petersen (2012, 77), rituals are "intentional ways of approaching a routine, with careful consideration of the needs of the individual within the routine. For early childhood professionals, they are a way to connect on a deeper level with families and their children." Teachers can use rituals and routines "to create secure environments that nurture relationships" (Gillespie & Petersen 2012, 77). The chart below illustrates the differences among routines, rituals, and traditions.

Routines	Rituals	Traditions
Routines are events that regularly occur in a certain order. Routines help children learn the order of what happens during the day and to know what comes next in a day. "**Routines** are repeated, predictable events that provide a foundationfor the daily tasks in a child's life" (Gillespie & Petersen 2012, 76).	"**Rituals** are procedures or routines that are infused with deeper meaning. They help make common experiences uncommon events" (Deal & Peterson 1999, 32). "**Rituals** can be defined as special actions that help us navigate emotionally important events or transitions in our lives as well as enhance aspects of our daily routines to deepen our connections and relationships" (Gillespie & Petersen 2012, 76).	**Traditions** are meaningful events or experiences that a class or program has created and that are expected to occur regularly. "**Traditions** are significant events that have a special history and meaning and that occur year in and year out. Traditions are a part of the history; they reinvigorate the culture and symbolize it to insiders and outsiders alike. They take on the mantle of history, carrying meaning on their shoulders. When people have traditions that they value and appreciate, it gives them a foundation to weather challenges, difficulties, and change" (Deal & Peterson 1999, 33).
For example The I Love You Dinner started as an alternative February celebration that emerged from the routine of having regular potluck dinners. It took the normal potluck dinner and made it something special.	**For example** The I Love You Dinner grew from the routine of potluck dinners. It became a ritual when the routine was personalized for a specific class. As a ritual, the goal of the I Love You Dinner was to connect the classroom community by creating a unique dinner prepared by children, using specific techniques and tools that included the singing of songs and a menu co-created with the children.	**For example** The I Love You Dinner became a tradition when it was repeated at the same time of the year, every year, for more than 15 years. The children, families, and teachers looked forward to the dinner every year.

In early childhood settings, the repetitive, cyclical, and predictable nature of rituals and traditions makes everyday classroom events meaningful and reassuring to children. Routines make life feel orderly and knowable. Rituals take that feeling a step further. The purpose of a ritual is not only understanding what to do and where to do it but also connecting with the people who are part of that ritual. Over time and with intention, rituals can evolve into traditions. When traditions are passed to others, they take on a life of their own, continuing with or without the person who initiated the tradition. For example, in Miriam's preschool, they have a ritual of singing

the "Good-Bye Song" at the end of the day. Miriam arranged for a baby to visit the class as part of a program on teaching empathy and kindness. One day, when it was time for the baby to leave, the children broke into the class's ritual good-bye song. They sang it softly to the baby as she left their room. The children repeated this ritual every time the baby came for a visit. Eventually, welcoming a visiting baby and saying good-bye developed into a tradition in that preschool classroom. What a lovely sense of connection for all!

Why Develop Rituals and Traditions?

Rituals and traditions are a central part of life, whether they involve how meals are shared or how major events and holidays are celebrated. Most individuals and families have rituals and traditions that are meaningful to them. Researchers have spent significant time studying and assessing the importance of how rituals and traditions can support families during difficult times or stressful moments (Spagnola & Fiese 2007). Similarly, rituals can help teachers support children during stressful times. For example, when 3-year-old Lucretia's mother began traveling on a regular basis for her job, Javier, Lucretia's teacher, reported that she was especially sad at nap times. He spoke with Lucretia's mom and suggested that she write a series of notes for him to read to Lucretia at the beginning of nap time. Once Lucretia realized this would be a regular ritual when her mom traveled, she would climb onto Javier's lap at nap time to hear her mother's note. The ritual of reading the note with Lucretia soothed her and connected her to her mother, who was far away, and to her teacher, who was nearby. This ritual became a regular part of Lucretia's nap time routine when her mother traveled.

For families, the benefit of rituals is clear. Dengel states:

> Research done at George Washington University's Family Research Center indicated that children fare better in households where ritual is established and preserved. . . . A nightly dinner ritual of setting the table together, sitting down as a family, discussing the day's events, or saying grace before the meal can slow down the hectic pace of today's families and provide a sense of meaning and order to the day. When family members are upset with each other, daily rituals can pull them back together and provide the setting for working out problems. (2000, 1)

In early childhood settings, rituals and traditions can make many of the same routines—eating, resting, gathering together, and saying hello and good-bye—more meaningful. These rituals and traditions can create bonds and build relationships that can contribute to a caring community. In these caring communities, children and adults are able to support one another, gain a sense of belonging, and share a sense of purpose.

Rituals and Traditions Connect Communities

Using rituals and traditions helps develop a warm, stable, secure environment in which children can grow, make social connections, learn together, and be engaged in the learning process (Hyson 2008). Many early childhood programs also emphasize "relating" by teaching empathy and kindness as key resources to develop community and prevent bullying (see Smith-Bonahue, Smith-Adcock, & Ehrentraut 2015). Levine (2003) defines classroom community as "a place where students feel safe both emotionally and physically, where they feel supported, and where they feel enthusiastic about the discoveries each new school day will bring. It is a place where the individual is honored and where a sense of interdependence is built into the culture" (p. 5). Levine believes that rituals and traditions can create "a culture of empathy" in a community. He states,

> Routines and rituals inherent to the classroom community serve to ground the class in a sense of predictability, belonging, and security. . . . Rituals take many forms. They can be quite simple—writing the daily schedule on the board each morning or playing a few notes on the kalimba to signify that it is time to move onto the next task. . . . Rituals help the class flow from moment to moment within each day while facilitating a sense of self-responsibility along with the sense of safety that comes from a shared predictable experience. (2003, 12)

Rituals and Traditions Foster a Sense of Belonging

Similarly, educator, author, and musician Bev Bos stresses the importance of rituals and traditions in her workshops for teachers and families. When asked at a workshop at Virginia Association for Early Childhood Education (VAECE) why we should create rituals and traditions in our classrooms and programs, she answered, "People need to experience a feeling of intimacy and a sense of belonging. We lead very busy lives and don't have many opportunities to connect with each other" (Bos 2013). Bev believes "belonging" is one of the cornerstones to building community. Rituals and traditions can create that sense of belonging.

Consider the following example. When 3-year-old Carlos joined his class, it was the first time he was cared for by anyone outside of his immediate family. At different times throughout the day, particularly at transitions, Carlos cried and asked for his mother. His teacher, Aileen, spoke with his family to create a ritual to soothe him. Carlos's mother told Aileen that she sang to Carlos to soothe him when he cried. Aileen now picks him up in her arms, rocks him, and sings "My Mommy Comes Back" to him, a song that reassures Carlos that his mother will always return. Aileen selected that song because she can sing it in Spanish, which is Carlos's home language. Aileen kisses Carlos on his forehead three times and says, "I will take care of you until your mommy comes back." This ritual helps ease Carlos's fears and connects him to his new preschool family.

Routine	Carlos was struggling with the transition from home to school, a transition that can be challenging.
Ritual	Aileen spoke with the family to decide how to help Carlos with the transition. Singing a special song in Spanish became the ritual.
Purpose Intentionality	The purpose of this ritual was to help Carlos transition from home to school while building a bond between Carlos and his teacher. The ritual helped Carlos feel that he was in a stable, caring environment with a teacher who understood and supported him. This included using his home language.
Personal Individualized	Aileen learned that Carlos's mother sings to him to soothe him. To comfort him in the classroom, she used a song she could sing in Spanish, his home language.
Tools Techniques	Aileen chose a song that had a message that was meaningful to the situation, "My Mommy Comes Back" by Hap Palmer. She hugged and rocked him and kissed his forehead three times.

Rituals and Traditions Create a Supportive Learning Environment

Children thrive and learn best in settings where they feel connected and safe. Building a community that includes children, teachers, and families contributes to that sense of safety. Establishing rituals and traditions is an effective way to build a sense of community and belonging.

Bailey states that in a school community that fosters connections, children will have increased willingness to learn, better impulse control, and overall increased and improved attention span (Conscious Discipline 2014). The school community is a foundation for success. It helps children feel connected and part of something. It gives them a sense of pride and ownership in their classroom and school life. It contributes to children growing and developing in a safe, secure learning community. According to Stewart (2013),

Everyday Rituals

Our individual lives are ordered and made meaningful with daily [routines] . . . the first cup of coffee, goodbye kisses, routes taken to school or work. . . . Ritual joins routine and the physical order as the secure skeleton that holds individuals and groups together in those times of stress, against the uncertainties of teachers and children who come and go. . . . These [rituals] are marked by symbolic acts that have great meaning and emotional power. Group daily rites [rituals]—i.e., sharing the same song and the same story day after day—reassure against the unknown void. Individual rituals between children and caregivers can become pinions of security—a special touch, a shared joke, any regularly shared exchange. (Greenman 1988, 122)

When I use the term "creating community" I am referring to that sense of belonging, of being a member of our team, of being someone we value in our classroom. I am referring to the idea that every child has something amazing to offer and can make a difference in our classroom. I am referring to how the set-up and look of my classroom will make children feel. And I am referring to how I will help my students feel genuinely connected to each other, to the teachers, to the environment, and to the processes we explore throughout each day. . . .

Teachers who build a sense of community foster children's sense of identity and connectedness. For example, when children recognize that the song they hear their teacher singing about pandas means it's time for them to go inside, they are identifying with the Panda Classroom. An adult who had Jacky as a preschool teacher still talks about being in the Dinosaur Classroom, a clear indication that Jacky fostered a sense of identity for the children in the room.

Fostering connections. Consistent rituals and traditions help children feel safe and supported, an essential component of a caring community. When teachers and directors in a program work with families to intentionally create rituals and traditions that families and children depend on, relate to, and connect with, they create a strong community that is united through shared rituals and traditions.

In high-quality preschool programs, people feel a strong sense of community. Families linger at the door to talk to teachers or directors about the day, an event, or significant moments. Children participate in good-bye rituals, celebrations, or other important events of the day. When families are engaged and respected for what they can contribute, such as sharing a family tradition with their child's classmates, the children see the mutual respect that the adults have for each other. They learn the importance of a strong and connected school community.

In this kind of community, teachers talk with one another to purposefully plan activities that foster connections. Teachers use rituals to ease separations at the beginning of the day and develop traditions that bring families, staff, and children together. "The School Family [community] builds connections between families

What a Director Can Do

How can directors inspire teachers to create rituals and traditions?

- **Reflect on what is important to you.** What are some important rituals in your life? What traditions matter most to you? What rituals and traditions do you remember from your childhood?

- **Start small.** Share a personal tradition with a class (read a special book from your childhood, share a song or skill like playing a musical instrument). Participate in a fun event, such as wearing a costume on Wacky Day, and inspire your community by being an active part of it. The children and teachers will love to see that side of you. Cook something special for a school potluck.

- **Create a comfortable space in your office** so families, children, and staff feel welcome. Perhaps offer a children's corner with books and toys or a space with big chairs and professional resources for teachers and families. If you set up your office so people feel comfortable in it, you will get to know them, connect with them, and find out what is important to them. You can create rituals and traditions once you understand the values of the people in your school community.

and schools, teachers and teachers, teachers and students, and students and students to ensure the optimal development of all" (Conscious Discipline 2014).

Welcoming families begins the moment they walk in the door. This includes the director's office. Kimberly is a center director whose office is located next to the front door of the center. She greets staff, children, and families as they walk into and out of school. She invites them into her office to say hello or good-bye, share ideas, repeat anecdotes, or just spend a moment together before beginning or ending the day. Children love to feed the fish in her aquarium and watch them swim around. She also maintains a corner with children's books, squishy gooey toys, paper and crayons, and games for children to play. Parents and teachers might also spend time squeezing a stress toy, sitting down, chatting, and connecting. Each room at the center also has a comfy corner with squishy toys, pets, and places for children to sit down and relax. At Kimberly's program, all the environments, from the entryway to the classroom to the director's office, are warm and inviting with a focus on building a sense of connectedness and community. Beginning or ending each day with feeding a fish during an office, visit or chatting with families, teachers, and children fosters the feeling that they are part of a school community.

This focus on building community from the director's office to the classroom creates a cohesive, overall sense of safety, caring, and connectedness. Using rituals as a tool to support a sense of connectedness may help children and families who are facing stressors. At home and in the community, children may experience challenges that you may not be aware of, so welcoming all children with open arms and providing a sense of security that days at school are predictable and filled with loving connections may help them through stressful times.

Like other families, school families are made up of different personalities and people with different strengths, likes, and dislikes. However, no matter how different people are, we all yearn to connect and belong.

As Imber-Black states, "Rituals have existed throughout time. They seem to be part of what it means to be human" (Imber-Black & Roberts 1992, xvii). In early childhood settings, connections created through rituals and traditions are as important as the environment, the curriculum, and the teachers. Teachers can use traditions like the I Love You Dinner, and administrators can use a welcoming atmosphere in their offices, to create a community that includes families, children, and teachers.

Why Use Rituals and Traditions to Build Community?

Because children spend many hours in group settings, it is increasingly important to provide an environment in which all children feel safe, secure, and connected to loving people. Young children especially need these connections and the sense of security and community they foster (Gillespie & Petersen 2012). Creating a classroom and program community, each with its own rituals and traditions, helps children and families feel they have a place where they belong.

> [The need] for structure and routine can be seen in many areas of our lives. . . . Classroom rituals and routines . . . help children to feel psychologically safe and comfortable in an unpredictable world. Most people, including children, are more at ease when they know what to expect during their day. It is stressful for all of us to be in settings in which we don't know what will happen next. This may be a great way to spend a few minutes on a roller coaster, but for daily work, it is unsettling and even frightening to children. Stable routines help children develop feelings of security, trust, and independence, and they serve as a protective factor against stressful family conditions. (Rand 2012)

Rituals and traditions are important for building community in early childhood settings because they

- Provide a caring, connected, and safe structure during transitions and difficult times
- Offer a personalized sense of familiarity and create shared values
- Order our lives in ways that connect the past, present, and future

1. Rituals and Traditions Provide a Caring, Connected, and Safe Structure During Transitions and Difficult Times

Preschool teachers help children through difficult times, which may include daily disagreements or a significant loss, such as a teacher leaving, a death, or changes in a family structure. Establishing rituals that serve as a source of healing benefits everyone. Bailey (2000) adds, "These rituals can ground children when change threatens them" (p. 14). Wright (2014) discusses the importance of rituals when working with children who have experienced trauma and stress: "There are no shortcuts to building trusting relationships and safe classroom environments that allow traumatized children to heal. Trust is lost much more quickly than it is recovered. However, fostering positive

relationships, supporting children's transitions to school, and creating a supportive learning environment might eventually make a difference" (91). Rituals can contribute to these positive relationships by providing "warm, caring, one-on-one interactions" (Wright 2014, 91). They help children bond and trust during a time when they are more vulnerable and disconnected. Rituals also add a meaningful dimension to routines, giving them a sense of security when children need it most.

Four-year-old Harry offers a poignant reminder about how rituals can provide security during difficult times. During the two years Harry was in preschool, the community coped with crises that included the 9/11 terrorist attacks and the sniper attacks in Montgomery County, Maryland. Harry began having bad dreams and expressed concern about being safe. In Jacky's preschool classroom, she had established several rituals to use when children had difficulty sleeping or when a child might feel powerless. The purpose was to help children feel safe, connected, and powerful. One was a chant that included hand motions. Harry was the smallest child (in stature) that year. He often felt afraid. Jacky worked with his family to address Harry's needs. She shared the chant that the children used in the classroom, hoping that Harry would use it at home too. His mother reported that at night, she would hear him in the next room repeating the power chant he had learned in preschool, "I'm brave, I'm strong, and I'm powerful!" Harry also knew if he still felt scared, the second part of this class ritual, finding people who help in a crisis, would soothe his fears. Harry began bringing his firefighter toy to school and walking it to each corner of the room. After the toy firefighter checked each area, Harry would call to the teacher, "Everything's clear here." The class would thank the firefighter for his brave help, and, of course, thank Harry, too!

Kersey and Masterson (2013) explain: "To form a sense of community, we want to engage children in positive experiences that support their security and well-being. Whether we work with infants, toddlers, or with children in preschool, kindergarten, or the early elementary years, creating a sense of belonging and safety is a priority" (p. 4).

2. Rituals and Traditions Offer a Personalized Sense of Familiarity and Create Shared Values

Roeser believes that intentional rituals in a classroom can teach children the value of kindness. Children struggle to regulate their emotions because they "haven't developed their prefrontal cortex, so they have trouble keeping in mind their best intentions… [their] working memory isn't fully developed" (Roeser 2014). One way to help children understand the importance of kindness is to "create rituals to remind children of their highest intentions" (Roeser 2014). In a class given for the Random Acts of Kindness Foundation, Roeser stated that when we provide children with calming and connecting rituals, like ringing a special chime, spending a moment of quiet on a carpet, or welcoming children each day with a ritual, we allow children to become present and connected to one another. "Kindness is a skill that can be practiced over time . . . like riding a bike. . . . [We] learn it so well it becomes automatic" (Roeser 2014).

As educators, we know that helping develop children's social and emotional skills is crucial preparation for life. Rituals of kindness are one way we can teach children to connect to one another. These rituals are one way to teach children empathy. Devon's class of 4-year-olds participates in the Random Acts of Kindness Week (see www.randomactsofkindness.org) in February. One ritual from that week that they have continued throughout the year is using a kindness basket. Devon's class has a specially decorated basket with paper hearts, crayons, markers, and stickers next to it. When any child in the class sees another child performing an act of kindness (fostering the children's social and emotional awareness), they ask the teacher to write it on one of the hearts (part of early literacy), and then place it in the basket. The child who recognizes the kind act will give a sticker to the classmate. At the end of the week, one child counts (a math skill) the hearts in the basket. On the last day of every month, they have a celebration, usually a pizza party, and talk about the kind acts that were recorded on each heart. Sometimes they invite families or another class to participate.

Routine	The class notes and celebrates Random Acts of Kindness week.
Ritual	The class has a kindness basket, counts hearts every Friday, totals for the month, has a party, and sings the same song.
Purpose Intentionality	The purpose of this ritual is to promote, notice, and celebrate kind acts.
Personal Individualized	Recording each child's ideas on hearts notes their thinking. In addition, a child can give a sticker to the child whose kind act he noticed.
Tools Techniques	The tools used are the basket, hearts, stickers, and a song the children sing.

3. Rituals and Traditions Order Our Lives in Ways That Connect the Past, Present, and Future

Rituals and traditions can create a sense that we are part of something bigger and better than ourselves. They make us feel safe because there are events and moments that we can always count on and look forward to. Children need to be able to predict and connect with the things that help them feel competent, safe, and secure. We often think of routines as a way for children and teachers to order their lives. This is true. However, turning routines into deeply meaningful and personal rituals and traditions can also define the history, culture, and community of an early childhood setting.

Children remember significant rituals and traditions. Galinsky asks, "What do you think your kids will remember most? That pricey family vacation to Disney World or the tea with toast and jelly you always made them when they were sick? Surprise: It's the tea and toast, or rather, the small, everyday routines that endure. . . . Even the simplest rituals make children (and parents) feel that they're a part of a unit, which is key to imbuing kids with a sense of security" (2001). Children remember the moments that happen again and again . . . the rituals that they can count on and make them feel safe and loved. Rituals and traditions can stay with them forever.

What Is the Value of Rituals for Adults and Children?

The following is based on "Ten Good Things Rituals Do for Children" (Cox 2012, 15). It shows that the benefits of family rituals can also apply to the value of creating community in an early childhood setting.

- Impart a Sense of Identity—For early childhood programs, identity can include bonding with the school or classroom as something special and unique, and gaining a sense of belonging to that group.

- Provide Comfort and Security—Early childhood professionals know that young children thrive best when they are in a program that is caring, safe, and secure, and where each child feels he or she belongs. Rituals and traditions repeated over time can create that kind of environment.

- Help to Navigate Change—Early childhood teachers navigate everyday transitions as well as transitions that may be unexpected, like water pipes bursting in winter or needing a substitute teacher. When there are established rituals that remind children the classroom is a safe, caring place to be, it can help everyone navigate changes.

- Teach Values—Classrooms incorporate the values, customs, cultures, and beliefs of children, teachers, and families. For example, rituals and traditions can be established that help teach kindness.

- Cultivate Knowledge of Cultural or Religious Heritage—Building bonds with families provides opportunities to understand, respect, and accept everyone as the children, families, and teachers learn about each other.

- Teach Practical Skills—Seemingly simple skills, such as learning good manners about eating snack or how to wash their hands, can be turned into fun, meaningful rituals.

- Solve Problems—Think about using rituals to solve an issue. When challenges or conflicts arise, having a song to sing or an "I have a good idea" classroom job or reading a special class book about problem solving can be invaluable.

- Keep Alive a Sense of Those Who Have Departed—In early childhood settings, many children leave at the end of the year. Sometimes children or teachers move during the year, or a member of the community might have a serious illness or die. Rituals and traditions may help children and adults cope with these life events.

- Create Wonderful Memories—When Jacky interviewed the families of children she taught, many of their memories were about the rituals and traditions she created, such as the funny song the children sang for hand washing or the traditional end-of-the-year picnic.

❖ ❖ ❖ ❖ ❖ ❖

In "Creating Community, Generating Hope, Connecting Future and Past: The Role of Rituals in Our Lives," Neugebauer writes

> Rituals which connect us to our past, rituals taught by one generation to the next may be cultural or religious, or they may be familial. There are also the rituals that we create because we want to say something about ourselves, about what we think is important, or because we want to create links. Wherever rituals originate, whether they have been part of us for a long time or short, they serve to identify us. They create community and a sense of belonging. They mark what we value as most important. They distinguish one group from another, one time period from another. They provide stability, consistency, and generate expectation and hope. Their anticipation leads us into the future. Their repetition connects us with the past. Their familiarity comforts us. (2000, 49)

Research and our own experiences show us the importance of rituals and traditions in our lives, as well as in the lives of children. Historically, these traditions and rituals were centered in family life. Because young children may spend up to 12,000 hours in early childhood settings (Isbell 2015), creating a place where they feel secure and safe is critical. The classroom is their home, and their peers and teachers are like a family at school. Rituals "strengthen the bond between parents and child as well as create a partnership between parents and their child's teacher" (Gillespie & Petersen 2012, 77). We can create this community and sense of security with rituals and traditions. We can create a strong, caring, connected community in early childhood settings by sharing important moments together and by intentionally connecting with children, families, and staff through rituals and traditions.

In the Next Chapter

How can you begin developing and building rituals and traditions at your early childhood setting? You may already have routines that can become rituals. How do you greet children in the morning? Is there a routine for saying good-bye at the end of the day? In the next chapter we will look at how you can use daily rituals to create meaningful connections.

Reflections

- What rituals and traditions do you remember from your own childhood?
- What rituals and traditions, if any, have you continued as an adult?
- Ten years from now, if you were to interview children and families from your program, what rituals and traditions would you like them to remember?

2

Transforming Daily Routines Into Meaningful and Intentional Rituals

Ms. Danielle, who teaches 3-year-olds, sits in the circle time area. As she begins to softly sing the class gathering song, the children make their way to the carpet. Once everyone has joined her, she reaches into the basket containing miniature pictures of the children mounted on tongue depressors. She takes one stick out at a time and sings that child's name. That child takes the stick and puts it into a pocket on the chart that lets everyone know who is in class that day. This is their beginning-of-the-day ritual that allows the children to see who is there that day. Then they greet each other and begin the day connecting as a group.

Ms. Danielle has transformed a daily circle time routine into a beginning-of-the-day ritual. To turn a routine into a ritual, William Doherty, author of *The Intentional Family*, suggests becoming intentional about planning rituals by signaling when they are to take place, being clear about what happens during the ritual, and signaling when the ritual is complete (Doherty 1999). For example, noon may be the time to eat lunch. That is the routine. It becomes a ritual when it starts with a song or chant that is meaningful to those who hear it and is unique to that group of children. Another example is the routine of saying good-bye to the children at the end of the day. When this routine includes a meaningful and personal interaction for the children in that particular class, the routine becomes a ritual. Jacky used to say to each child, "See ya, wouldn't want to be ya, I wanna be me." This silly good-bye turned into a ritual of leaving because it was a moment of connection with each child. Routines help everyone know what is expected, but rituals offer more than simply knowing what will happen on any given day. Creating meaningful and personal rituals from routines can transform transitions and challenging times, as well as everyday moments, into opportunities for connection and community building.

What Are the Key Elements of a Ritual?

Cox (2012), Atlas (2005), and Biziou (2000) describe the key elements of family rituals. Teachers can apply these same elements—intentionality, individualization, and use of specific techniques or tools—to transform everyday actions and routines into meaningful rituals.

1. Intentionality. Ask yourself what you want to achieve by creating a ritual. What are you hoping children, teachers, and families will experience or gain from this ritual? For example, you may feel that it is important to have a routine of greeting children and families when they arrive in the morning. If you create a ritual that turns those greeting times into times of special connection, it communicates that the classroom is a special place to be, a place where everyone gathers together in caring ways. Developing a welcoming ritual is one way to start this process.

2. Individualization. When rituals have special meaning to the people involved, they are effective for that group. Part of creating rituals is adding elements that specifically relate to the children you teach. For example, Tina, who teaches 4-year-olds in a program that values kindness and friendship, uses a transition song about being friends. Tina and the children wrote a friendship song that they used for the entire year!

3. Tools and Techniques. Young children learn best when they are involved in active, hands-on experiences that engage their senses and are repeated over time. Using objects like a special puppet, the sounds of a familiar chant or song, or a special sound like a soothing bell to mark the beginning or ending of a time together helps the children connect with the ritual. Select a tool or technique that makes the ritual unique and meaningful to the children.

In *Super Teaching: Over 1000 Practical Strategies*, Jensen talks about the different aspects of rituals. He states that teachers can personalize a ritual by considering ways that children can actively participate in the ritual. For example, a teacher might blow a train whistle to signal that it is time to begin a routine—getting ready to go outside. Adding an opportunity for the children to respond with "All Aboard" or "Train leaving the station" actively engages them in the ritual (Jensen 2009).

The examples in this chapter and elsewhere in the book use the key elements of intentionality, individualization, and tools and techniques. You can use the ideas as written or use them as models for creating rituals for the children you teach.

Daily Rituals

Daily routines include eating snack or meals, taking naps, washing hands after playing outdoors, and so on. When children transition from one time of the day to another, such as during morning drop-off, they sometimes need extra comfort and encouragement. The rituals you develop around daily routines and transition times may last for only one year or may become something that you use for years to come. Daily routines that can become rituals include

- Morning greeting
- Meals
- Transitions
- Nap time
- Coping with challenges
- Good-byes

In addition to the three key elements of rituals mentioned on page 20, Cox suggests having a clear beginning and end to the ritual and connecting the ritual to an action (2003). For example, if you are creating a cleanup ritual, the **intention** is to focus children's attention on cleaning up. The **individual** aspect can be the unique way you introduce the cleanup process to that group of children. The **tool** you use may be a sound or a puppet. In Cecilia's classroom, she signals that it is time for cleanup by playing chimes, then calls the children over to the circle time rug with a special puppet. She uses a tool that is unique to this classroom—Ivan the puppet—to assign each child a job. The children hug the puppet and move on to begin cleaning. He is a unique puppet with a history and life developed by the teacher (Corbey-Scullen & Howell 1997). There is also a beginning, an end, and an action to this ritual.

When you connect rituals to routines, and they happen on a consistent basis, children can begin to count on the rituals as well as benefit from the connections they create. Rituals become fun and unique ways to work through different times of the day, helping children and adults complete routines with less stress. Rituals can be created not only by the teachers but also by the children. They can bond children with one another and with adults, while creating a place of safety and security. They may be planned or come about spontaneously.

How to Begin Creating Rituals

Daily routines, such as hitting snooze three times before getting out of bed, exercising for 30 minutes, or parking in the same spot every day, provide meaningful structure and organization to your day. For a routine to become a ritual, it must have the key elements of intentionality, individualization, and tools or techniques. Rituals are intentional and meaningful, designed for a specific child or group, and use tools or techniques specific to that ritual. It isn't simply having coffee because you need the caffeine in the morning; it is the time you take to make the coffee, using special coffee cups, maybe ones you've had for years while you sit and drink it at the kitchen table and touch base with your spouse about what the day holds. Drinking coffee is not the ritual. The time savoring the coffee in those cups, connecting with the person across the table, and hugging at the end of morning coffee is what turns it into a ritual.

Classroom Identity

To begin building community using rituals and traditions, one place to start is to establish a classroom identity.

Give the class a name. Some classroom labels can feel cold and impersonal. Children, staff, and families benefit by being part of a school community. Developing a name for the class is a way to create a specific identity that defines that unique group. Identify what you think is fun and exciting and bring your interests into the class in a way that the children can relate to. For example, in Jacky's former program every class had to come up with a name starting with a different letter of the alphabet. Her class had to start with D, and because she knows a great deal about dinosaurs and because children love them, they chose to become the Dinosaurs. Jacky and the children developed many rituals based on the class name. For example, Jacky sang a song about dinosaurs when it was time to go inside. Each child knew the dinosaur song by heart, and they all knew that when they heard the dinosaur song it was time to come together as a class. Jacky used this song for so many years as the "going inside" ritual that it became a tradition in the Dinosaur classroom.

Hello and Welcome

Morning greeting is an important time for a ritual. The following are ideas that you can use as your morning ritual or as a model for creating your own good-morning ritual to use with your class. If you have some children who struggle with this transition, you may want to develop morning rituals for those children.

Start Your Day Off Right

Many of us are rushed in the morning, making sure lunch is packed, permission slips are signed, and children have their homework. Not only is it important to start your day with a good breakfast, it is also important to start your day with a ritual of connection.

Before you welcome the children to another day together, stop, take a deep breath, and find your own personal positive thinking that will help you build connections throughout the day. Jacky often listened to upbeat music on the way to work and would come into the classroom singing one of the songs. Select welcome songs to play as the families drop their children off each morning. Choose a song that reflects your likes and interests and those of the children. You might play relaxing classical music or jam into the classroom singing "Dancing in the Streets" by Martha Reeve and the Vandellas.

Meet each child at the door and offer him or her a high five, a handshake, a kiss, a hug, or a wink. If you have a class pet, each child could greet him, blow him a kiss, and wish him well. These rituals will help you start the day with a moment of connection, allowing children to feel safe and cared for as they begin a new day of playing and learning with their classmates.

Morning greeting. Welcoming children at the beginning of the day sets the tone for the rest of the day. Children should walk into the classroom and feel as though you are looking forward to their arrival. Add to the routine you already have by taking an extra minute or two to connect with each child, making each child feel welcome. Becky Bailey suggests a ritual that she calls "A Wonderful Woman Who Lived in a Shoe." Hold a child's hands and touch each finger while saying, "There was an old woman who lived in a shoe, she had so many children, she knew exactly what to do. She held them. She rocked them. And tucked them in bed. I love you, I love you, is what she said" (Bailey 2000). Then press the child's hands against his chest and give him a hug. This takes one to two minutes, creating a moment of connection with each child.

Hello/good-bye window. A ritual created at Kimberly's center is the hello/good-bye window. Children are often sad when their parents leave for work so the center turned a large picture window near the entrance into a hello/

good-bye window. The children can stand at the window and wave good-bye to their parents in the morning and greet them at the end of the day (see photo). At the beginning of the school year, teachers read *The Hello, Goodbye Window*, by Norton Juster, to the children. They talk with the children about saying good-bye to their parents in the morning with the understanding that their parents will return at the end of the day. Sometimes a teacher needs to hold a child in her arms so that she can wave good-bye because the child just cannot bring herself to let go of her parent. Some teachers add a stool next to the window so all children can reach the window and see through it clearly. Choose a window that is convenient for you and your children to use for this ritual. In Kimberly's center, there is a window in the main recreational space so all children have access to it in the morning. Other centers may have a hello/good-bye window in classrooms or drop-off areas. In Jacky's classroom, one parent built a platform with steps that reached up to the window so children could see out the window and wave good-bye to their parents. Teachers also explain the importance of the window to families so they understand that when they walk out of the door, they should turn around and say good-bye to their child who is waiting at the window. It is a ritual that has become a tradition. It is comforting to families and children alike and allows each day to get off to a loving start.

Two ears, two eyes, and a belly button. You can also greet each child by asking him what he brought to school that day and then laugh together as you point out the two ears, two eyes, and belly button the child brought (see "What did you bring to school today?" in Bailey 2000). Depending on the child, you can become sillier until you are both laughing. This is more than a routine. This meaningful ritual connects you and the child and welcomes the child into the classroom where he is part of the school community.

Hello ritual. Sonia, who teaches 3-year-olds, uses a sign on her door as part of a hello ritual. The sign describes four choices of being greeted: a hug, handshake, high five, or smile. Each child chooses a greeting. (Sonia says that the children love to be the greeter!) In addition, Sonia tapes a hopscotch pattern on the floor. When each child comes into the room, he walks or jumps his way into the room. Even the families like to hopscotch their way into the classroom!

Songs and Chants

Another way to welcome children at the beginning of the day or to signal a transition is through songs and chants.

Greeting song. You might use songs and chants that have special meaning for your class, or create one using a simple tune like "Row, Row, Row Your Boat." Bev Bos sings "We've Been Waiting for You," a song written by the late Tom Hunter, to greet children as they come into her program every day. Sing or chant this simple, short, and loving welcome song (or any other welcome song that reflects your interests and those of the children you teach) to each child as she walks through the door.

Snacks and Meals

"In some cultures, the simple ceremony of sharing a meal with someone makes you part of the tribe" (Cox 2012, 36). Most early childhood programs have snack and mealtimes as part of their daily routine. Transforming this routine into a ritual can make it a special time that contributes to each child's sense of feeling part of the group. The following ideas turn the routine of snacks and meals into a ritual.

Hand washing. A simple activity like hand washing can become a meaningful ritual if it is individualized for each child. Gillespie and Petersen discuss how hand washing can be a connecting moment. "For example, a caregiver engaged in the routine of hand washing with Bobby (10 months) sings the ABC song to him, so that Bobby washes his hands for the required 30 seconds. She uses this song because it is the song Bobby's mother uses at home. For Eric, 30 months, she sings a song about the bubbles going down the drain, a ritual they developed together to make that 30 seconds fly by. These simple rituals around hand washing help deepen her relationship with each child and make even the mundane meaningful for both child and adult" (Gillespie & Petersen 2012, 77). Adding meaning to everyday interactions with children creates rituals that can build a caring community.

Eating together. Mealtimes can be challenging because there is often a limited amount of time for children to wash hands, eat, clear the table, and prepare to go home or for nap time. But you can reframe mealtime. It can be a time to connect with children by engaging them in conversation. Before creating a mealtime ritual, take a moment to think about what meals mean to you.

For example, when Jacky was growing up, Friday pizza dinners with her family were special meals. As she grew older, she stayed up late chatting with her parents and her sisters at the end of what often were busy weeks. Everyone in the family looked forward to Friday night meals. It was a ritual that brought the family together. Her sister still maintains the tradition of Friday pizza nights, even when her daughter comes home from college on visits. For Jacky, family meals are a time for conversation and connection. What does mealtime mean to you?

In one preschool program, Sarai wants the 4-year-olds she teaches to learn about each other. At lunch time, she introduces a fun discussion topic using a game she calls Our Special Lunch Time Questions. The class has discussed questions from "What do zoo animals do after all the people leave?" to "If you uncovered a treasure box on our playground, what do you think might be inside?" The children who want to chat look forward to sharing their thoughts and ideas, and Sarai notes that the children often hang around the table after they have finished eating to continue these conversations. The children who want to focus on eating peacefully simply do so. They often just sit and listen or nod their heads and smile.

Elegant snack day. Another ritual to make snack and mealtimes meaningful as well as build a sense of community is "elegant snack day." Tymika, a preschool teacher, was inspired by her own formal Sunday dinners as a child to create a snack time ritual. Each Friday, she and the children cover the snack table with a tablecloth, sometimes add electric candles, and always use real plates, cups, and silverware. Families take turns bringing in the tableware and even adding fresh flowers to the tables. Tymika and the children look forward to Friday snack times, their favorite time of the week. Elegant snack days often last longer than other snack times. Everyone sits at the beautiful table and enjoys their time together.

Mealtime Conversation Ideas

1. What is your favorite food that you like to eat for dinner?

2. If a dinosaur came to where you live, what would you do or say?

3. Who lives in a castle? When you think about the people who might live in a castle, who would you like to be friends with?

4. If any animal could come and live with you, what animal would you choose?

5. If you found some money on the playground, what would you do?

6. If a new friend came to our classroom, what could you say that would make him or her be glad to be part of our class?

7. Sing a song that you like.

8. What is your favorite character (you might need to explain what "character" means) from a book?

9. Tell us about a time you did something fun with your family.

10. What is your favorite thing to do in our classroom?

Try something new. Sometimes rituals can make a somewhat mundane activity new and interesting. Maybe it creating a "seat of the day" that has something special taped to it. Think of a system where children are selected— be it alphabetical by first name or by birthday. Juanita, who teachers 4-year-olds, uses this ritual once a week. On Friday, the children know that there will be a surprise taped under one seat. Juanita selects children alphabetically by first name. For each child, she selects a roll of stickers that reflects the interests of that child. For example, when it was Aisha's turn, Juanita taped a roll of horse stickers to her chair because Aisha likes horses. Juanita includes enough stickers so the child can share the stickers with the other children her table. Another ritual could be a surprising "eat snack outside" day. Something as simple as eating a meal or snack outside on blankets (even in the snow!) can make it special.

Mealtimes may be stressful because you are trying to balance many tasks at the same time. Adding a ritual slows the pace, creates ways to share time together, helps reduce the stress, and turns an everyday routine into something special.

Transitions

Every day includes many transitions, from play to cleanup to lunch to nap to outdoor play and back inside. Rituals can help children anticipate and prepare for transitioning to the next activity. You may have a song that you sing when it is time to clean up, or maybe you chime a bell to gain the children's attention. Although these are good techniques for transitions, personalizing them for the children you teach is an opportunity to build community.

Jump on the train. Alejandro walks out of the door with a cabasa, a rhythm instrument, and begins to shake it, making sounds like a train going "choo choo." He then begins to sing one of his favorite songs, "Pufferbellies" by Sharon, Lois, and Bram. The 4-year-olds start to dance and sing along with him. They then turn into different cars of a train and link up, putting their hands on the shoulders of the child in front of them, to transition to the next activity of the day, such as going outside, coming back inside, or going to the bathroom to wash their hands before snack. Even at the end of the school year, the children still eagerly jump on that train, often calling out the names of train cars as they link together and say, "All aboard our train!"

Clap, sing, chant, and dance. Layla loves to dance and sing with the 3-year-olds she teaches. She plays music so the children can dance their way into cleanup time. She has used "Oh My Goodness Look at This Mess!" from Sweet Honey in the Rock to traditional songs about cleanup. Layla and the children clap, sing, and dance their way to each area of the room that needs to be cleaned up. Often Layla weaves instructions into the tune of the song to help children focus on what needs to be cleaned up next.

Layla also uses songs and chants when the children have to transition from inside to outside or back inside. She chants directions to a beat and the children join right in. One of her favorites is a chant by Billy B. about a line needing a leader (see http://billybproductions.com/lyrics-a-line-needs-a-leader/). She uses his chant and then adds her own lines to the chant to engage the children. This ritual helps Layla and the children connect with shared joy and laughter during a time of day that otherwise might be tedious.

Follow the magic dot. Cliff helps the 4-year-olds he teaches get ready for a transition by "following the magic dot." Using a high-powered flashlight, Cliff projects a bright round dot on the floor for the children to follow. When it is circle time, for example, the children use a special chant to follow the dot to the circle time rug. Often that silly dot ends up on the ceiling and the children laugh together, knowing they are not ceiling walkers!

Chime. Miriam understands that engaging the senses, such as when she chimes a bell or slowly dims the lights, is an effective way to gain children's attention. This signals the 4-year-olds she teaches that they have five minutes to finish what they are doing before it is time for the next activity.

Silly sounds, chants, and props can engage children both playfully and meaningfully, helping children feel that they are seen and known. Choose the tools and techniques that connect with the interests of the children as well as what the children are learning. The rituals you develop make transition times go more smoothly, and they add a bit of fun!

All of these transition activities incorporate the elements of a ritual—they are intentional, use tools created by teachers or with children, and are unique for each classroom. What ideas will work with the children you teach? Do you have a favorite song to sing, dance, and clap to while cleaning up? How can you modify these ideas to work with the children you teach?

Nap Time

Some children have a difficult time settling down at nap time. Naps often occur after lunch, a time when children are talkative and social, so they need a way to slow down before sleeping. Setting up a relaxing environment and using soothing rituals can help children ease into nap time and make the process less stressful for everyone. Some teachers begin by turning out one light or dimming the lamps or lights in the room. Andrea, a pre-K teacher, "blows" out the lights with dramatic flair as she whispers, "Good night, lights," letting the children know the room will soon grow dark.

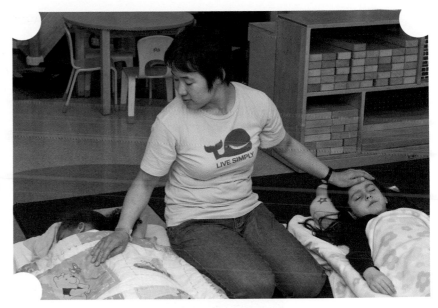

Form small groups. In Ana's class, the 4-year-olds are divided into two small groups before they lie down on their cots. Each group is led by a teacher, each with its own ritual. In Ana's group the children pass around a basketful of stones. Each child picks one stone to hold. Then they pass the basket around again. Each child holds his stone and says something positive that happened that morning. The children say things like, "I had fun with [names another child] in blocks today. I hope we can build together after nap time," or "I laughed so much this morning my belly was hurting. It was a fun morning!" then puts his stone in the basket and passes it to the next child. Ana guides the children carefully on how to say positive things, and ends by playing a small chime and sharing some thoughts of her own. Meanwhile, in the other group, Eric plays his guitar quietly and sings softly with the children. After their small group rituals are over, each child climbs into his cot and is tucked in by a teacher. Ana and Eric create a lovely and soothing atmosphere for the beginning of nap time.

Soothing spray. Some of the 3-year-olds that Cecelia teaches need help relaxing at nap time. She uses a special spray mist from a bottle of lavender-scented water. As the children lie down on their beds, she moves slowly and quietly around the room. She asks each child, "Would you like a sweet dreams spray?" Children who say yes get a quick spritz under their cot and then are surrounded with a lovely, relaxing scent. Cecelia and the children enjoy this nap time ritual.

Transforming Daily Routines

Sleepy lotion. Devon uses another way to help a child relax before resting or sleeping. He walks around the room after the children are lying down and offers to rub sleepy lotion on their temples or their arms. (Any lotion can work, but lavender or chamomile is ideal if scented products are not a concern.) He kneels at each child's cot and asks, "Ready for your magical sleepy lotion?" As in Cecilia's class, children have the option to refuse, yet most children eagerly look forward to time to connect with Devon and welcome the soothing touch and smell of the lotion.

Routine	Relaxing and preparing for nap time
Ritual	The class prepares for nap by lying on cots and rubbing sleeping lotion on their temples.
Purpose Intentionality	The purpose of this ritual is to allow the children to take a deep breath, relax, and be connected with a teacher or friend.
Personal Individualized	The teachers choose a soothing scent, and the individual children choose if they want the lotion. Even if they do not, many relax after the teacher spends a moment talking quietly with them.
Tools Techniques	The tool is the use of the scented lotion to relax the children.

Read a book. Nicole remembers being read to before going to asleep. A ritual she chose for nap time in her classroom is to read one chapter from a chapter book to the children as they lie down on their cots. She often picks her favorite books from childhood, like *Mr. Popper's Penguins* or *Pippi Longstocking*, or she reads a book about a topic the children are learning about or that reflects the interests of one or more of the children. She starts the reading ritual by saying, "Lie comfy on your bed; get ready to hear a special story being read." The 4-year-olds snuggle down on their cots, eager to hear the next chapter of the story. Nicole leaves the book out for children to look at after nap time. She often rereads the same chapter at circle time in case some children fell asleep before the end of the chapter.

Sleepy time song. Listen each day to the same sleep song, such as Jack Hartmann's "Everyone Needs to Rest" or a song that reflects your interests or those of the children. Cecilia plays this song for the children as they prepare for nap time. In addition to the song, Cecilia does a simple finger play in which she touches her nose, her head, her toes with the first chorus. She then physically connects with each child as she walks from cot to cot and gently touches his or her nose, head, and toes, a ritual preparing the children to calm all parts of their body and rest. Each child waits patiently for a turn.

Breathe deeply to relax. Deep breathing can help children relax before nap. Ask the children to hold up their two fists in front of their faces with their thumbs pointing up. Have them "smell" a flower (take a deep breath) as they inhale over one thumb and then "blow out the candle" (exhale) as they blow out deeply over the other thumb. Repeat three times. This helps children learn how to breathe in and out and calm their bodies. This is a ritual you can do with individual children to give them a moment with you that helps them transition to nap time.

Gentle wake-up. Some children need time and a waking time ritual to prepare for the next part of the day. If you have been playing soft instrumental music during nap time, you might change the music to something more upbeat, turn on flickering electric candles during the last 15 minutes to increase the light in the room in a soothing way, or play a wake-up song to cue the children that they have five minutes before it is time to get up. Or chime a subtle gong like they do in yoga and calmly tell the children to wiggle their toes, stretch their legs, give themselves a hug, and nod their heads before opening their eyes.

Once all the children are moving, you can put on a more energetic song, like "Wake Up Song" by Lisa Loeb, which will get the children moving and stomping their feet. The song is intentionally timed to let children know that it's time to get up. Choose your music specifically to match the interests of the children. If it takes a while for them to get up, they might need a mellow, relaxing song to come out of sleep. If they are ready to move when they wake up, they might enjoy an energetic song to wake up to and get going. Or the group might need both. Identify a song that is special to the children and that inspires them to get up and get going.

Think of the many rituals you can develop for nap time transitions and the tools you can use—from a chant to a spray to a song to deep breathing—that help children feel calm, soothed, and safe before resting or sleeping and when waking up from nap time.

Rituals for Challenging Times

One way to comfort an upset child, help resolve conflicts, or handle stressful events is to use a ritual. Bailey describes four components of connecting through rituals as eye contact, touch, presence, and a playful setting (2011, 201). According to Bailey, if you include these components in the ritual, you increase the chance of being able to connect to a child in a meaningful, profound way. Boyes says, "Due to the consistent structure they provide, rituals can be especially useful in managing a classroom peacefully and positively. This structure gives students a sense of stability and security, which in turn helps them to feel calm and competent in the classroom" (2006, 17).

Grumpy duster. When Ryan's mother asked him how she could help him feel better when he is cranky he said, "You need to get a grumpy duster to dust the grumpies off. That is what Ms. Carmen and Mrs. Abigail do at school." His teachers use a soft duster to very lightly brush or tickle children to help their grumpies go away. This ritual incorporates all four of Becky Bailey's principles to help a child in distress: physical touch, presence, eye contact, and a sense of playfulness. The ritual is so important to 3-year-old Ryan that he wanted to use it at home. The ritual created a bridge that connected his school to his home.

Puppet pals. Kaitlyn uses puppet pals to help the 3-year-olds she teaches cope with stressful times. Originally she used a Chester the Raccoon puppet from *The Kissing Hand,* by Audrey Penn, to welcome children into their new classroom at the beginning of the year. Every day, Chester gives each child a hug. When Tito struggled to separate from his dad in the morning, Kaitlyn used a special fuzzy cat puppet named Sammy who would greet him. Kaitlyn told Tito that Sammy missed his dad too and needed an extra hug. Tito would give this fuzzy cat a big hug and then carry him around the room until Tito was ready to play. Kaitlyn and the other teachers at that program soon learned that using puppets can help children get through challenging moments. To connect with children, they needed additional characters, so a dog, kitten, another raccoon, a squirrel, and many other friends have joined Chester. They all have names and a special tree home that Kaitlyn created with the children. Children sometimes nap with a puppet pal or take one home for a visit. Kaitlyn uses the puppets to talk with the children about their thoughts and feelings.

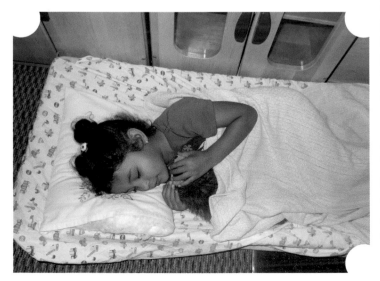

Each puppet pal has become an important part of this classroom's program. (Ideas for talking to children with puppets can be found in *A Show of Hands: Using Puppets With Young Children* [Crepeau & Richards 2003].)

Comfy corner. Sarai created a comfy corner where children can go to relax. The corner has headphones with calming instrumental or meditation music that can help children when they feel stressed. Also in the corner is a basket with toys to squeeze, pull, and press. Stress toys that are filled with water, gel, sand, and foam are durable and calming. Sometimes Sarai offers small containers of bubbles and wands. In addition to enjoying blowing bubbles, children need to take deep breaths when they blow bubbles, which can help them relax. Sarai sometimes uses this special place when she needs a quiet moment or time to take deep breaths and relax, modeling for the children how to relax. Sarai also asks each family to make a recording of something loving and soothing to their child. The children can listen to the recordings when they feel the need. The comfy corner has pictures showing four ways to relax, using a combination of yoga and relaxation activities. In Sarai's class, the children made their own book of ideas for relaxing. Having a comfy corner in and of itself can be soothing for children, yet it is adding the rituals that makes it intentional and personal for the children.

Feel better friend. Inspired by the work of Becky Bailey, Javier has a Feel Better Friend as a classroom job. Each week it is one child's job to help others feel better by providing hugs, Band-Aids, or tissues. This gives every child in the class the opportunity to care for one another and connect with their classmates. It is different from the job of table setter or door holder because it builds bonds among the children, helps them learn empathy, and fosters an atmosphere in which children can work well with one another. One ritualized part of this job is that the child asks, "How can I help you feel better? Would you like a lovey, a tissue, or a Band-Aid?" Each child who has the job can add to the ritual questions, yet the basic structure remains the same.

Special classroom jobs. Javier has developed many jobs that focus on being helpful and building relationships with each other. When he attended a workshop by Becky Bailey at an NAEYC conference in 2013, she shared the idea of creating jobs that are prosocial and offer opportunities for connection (Bailey 2011). One special job is the Idea Person. The child who is the Idea Person wears a special hat with a lightbulb pictured on it or a special flashing light attached. When there are conflicts or problems, this child can be called upon to help problem solve and contribute good

ideas. The ritual saying in this job is, "I have good ideas. How can I help you?"

Another job is the Morning Greeter, who greets all the children when they arrive by offering a smile, high five, hug, or sticker. The greeter says, "Welcome to our class. I came to say hello. Choose your favorite way!" Wearing a special apron or shirt with the options printed on it make the ideas visible as well as fun! Adding rituals to classroom jobs, particularly those that build community, contributes to fostering a classroom community that goes beyond typical responsibilities. All of the jobs have a ritual piece, usually an item children wear to perform their job or a saying or question. The saying or question might be one used together as a class or developed by the child who is doing the job for the week.

End the Day and Say Good-Bye

After being separated from their children all day or for a few hours, family members can feel as if they have missed out on their children's day and feel disconnected from them. Welcoming family members back at the end of the day and sharing information about their children's day is an important aspect of creating a community. Children also need a way to end their day and reconnect with their family.

Digital photo frame. Throughout the day Cliff takes photographs of the 4-year-olds he teaches. Near the end of the day, he loads the card from his camera into a digital picture frame that shows all the photos from that day. When families and children look at the photos together, the children can share their favorite memories or talk about the day's events on the way home. The photos give families a concrete way to stay connected to what happens each day.

Photo board. Latisha, who teaches pre-K, prints a few photos each day and attaches them to a poster board along with a meaningful quote of the day. She uses the quote, along with information about what the children are doing in the photos, to inspire and educate. Sometimes Latisha has children describe what they are doing and writes the children's words on the poster board. She hangs the poster board near the exit so family members see what happened that day. At pickup time, families look at the photos, descriptions, and quote. This helps them understand what their children do every day and lets the children revisit and talk about the day's activities. One parent has developed a ritual of sitting with a snack she brings for her daughter, looking at the pictures together, and talking about her child's day before their long drive home. This ritual makes the transition easier at the end of a long day as well as informs families about what children are learning and experiencing during the day.

Hello/good-bye window. The same window used for good-byes in the morning (see p. 24) becomes the hello window at the end of the day. The children sit at the window watching the world outside as they wait for their families to pick them up. At Kimberly's center, the children look out the window and call out to the family member who is arriving. One child told Jacky that the sign that said Good-Bye Window needed to be changed to Hello and Good-Bye Window, which he then helped create and hung over the window!

Closing song. At the last circle time of the day, Tina sings "The Time That We Have Been Together," a song by Bev Bos, Tom Hunter, and Michael Leeman. The song is a special way to mark the end of the day with the children. After the song ends, Tina and the preschoolers talk about what they want to remember about the day. This is a time when the teachers and children can reflect on their day together and what they might remember about it that they would like to share with their families. The song and discussion help children with the end-of-the-day transition. Sometimes families join the circle time with Tina and the children to hear the discussion. This ritual is one that Tina thinks may grow into a tradition for her!

It Takes Time

Creating a ritual takes time. It can take three weeks to develop a consistent routine, and it takes more time to turn that routine into a meaningful ritual. Consider the key elements of a ritual (see p. 20) of intentionality, tools and techniques, and individualization. If the ritual is important to you, if it is important to children and for children, stick with it! Do it again and again and again. The benefits of rituals are long term. They could be the beginning of a trusting and loving relationship between you and a child, among the children, between the children and their families, and between you and the children's families. "The bonds and memories created are an important benefit of creating rituals" (Atlas 2005, xiv).

"We are what we repeatedly do" (Durant [1961] 2006, 96). If this is true, then our day-to-day rituals become a part of us and those around us. Shouldn't we intentionally do things to strengthen our ties to children, families, one another, and our community? Daily rituals are critical for connecting people, creating school families, and strengthening the success of early childhood programs. Daily moments can be moments of connection. Imagine what you can do in a month!

What a Director Can Do

How can a busy director find time to share daily rituals with children, staff, and families? It seems almost impossible! But, it is possible. The following are ideas that might change your center culture forever:

- Open your door at the end of the day. Encourage children and families to stop by to say good-bye. They may want to chat about their day. It is a great way to get to know families in an informal manner.

- Invite groups of two to four children to your office once a week. Read them a story, let them play with the squishy toys in your office, or encourage them to explore art materials. Take this opportunity to learn about the children.

- Identify what you love or find interesting and share it with the children and staff. Kimberly is fascinated by bugs. When she goes outside once a week, the children know it is bug-watching time. They collect digging sticks and go on searches for bugs in the dirt. Because Kimberly does this regularly, when the children see Kimberly on the playground, they know the ritual of bug hunts has begun. You can also share your favorite song or type of music, bring in your favorite story to read with children, do a funny dance to say good-bye to each class at the end of the day, or share anything else that you like to do.

- Talk with families or send them short messages if you notice something unique or funny that their child said or did. Do the same for teachers and staff when you recognize something special about them. For example, Kimberly's center has a Star Board in the foyer with photos of everyone who works at the center. There are box of markers, cutout stars, and tape. Families or teachers can quickly grab a star and write a note, a thought, or a funny comment and hang it on the Star Board. It allows peers, parents, and supervisors to write notes of recognition and kindness. Everyone can read the notes, creating a point of connection and appreciation for the whole center. You can also privately recognize teachers' work with quick notes and cards in their mailboxes. Even a short text message of gratitude will go a long way. It is amazing what a few words and the time spent noticing will do to make a teacher feel special.

Rituals should be special and important to you. If they are, they will build memories with those around you.

Many programs already have routines that help children, staff, and families plan their days. These routines can be transformed into meaningful rituals by adding the three key elements of a ritual: *intentionality, individualization,* and *tools and techniques*. Rituals are created intentionally, so it is important to figure out the purpose of your ritual. Is it to help connect with a child, create a sense of security during a difficult time, bond with the families in your school, or another purpose? Once you determine the purpose, you can choose the tool that fits best, like a song, an event, or a staff bonding experience. The ritual should be personal, relevant, and possibly even quirky. What you build should relate to you, your community, the children, and their families. The ritual should mean something to you and the children in your class. Using this method, you can create rituals that stand the test of time and allow adults and children to connect, learn, and grow.

In the Next Chapter

The next chapter describes and outlines ways daily rituals can turn into weekly and monthly rituals. In addition, the chapter will examine how to create rituals that may turn into weekly or monthly traditions.

Reflections

Think about your daily routine.

- Name three times of day when you have established your own unique rituals.
- What songs do you remember from your childhood? Consider using some of these songs during transitions or at the beginning of mealtime or nap time.
- Many of us have bedtime rituals—a glass of water on the bedside table, a pillow we cannot sleep without, or a TV show we watch every night before we go to bed. We may remember books being read to us as a child before we went to bed. Think of how you can use some of your bedtime rituals to make nap time a soothing time for children.

3

Transforming Weekly and Monthly Routines Into Meaningful and Intentional Rituals

After a long weekend, 4-year-old Freddy slowly walks into the classroom. As soon as he opens the door he hears "ABC" by the Jackson 5, the welcome song for his class. Around the room he sees sensory options: potions, mixtures, slime, and clean soap dough. Freddy hurries now, remembering that it is Hands-On Monday, the day of week when he can feel different textures, smell lavender, hear his favorite welcome song, and enjoy starting the week with a soothing and sensory Welcome to the Week ritual.

Chapter 2 described ways to turn existing daily routines into meaningful rituals. This chapter outlines how to transform weekly schedules and monthly events into intentional rituals that foster a sense of belonging and a sense of community, creating an environment that supports children's learning and development (Hyson 2008).

Maloney said, "Ritual is basic to life in the classrooms and, as such, gives shape and form to that life" (2000, 149). Think about what you do to celebrate the start and end of your busy week. Do you end your week with a relaxing cup of tea, a movie, or time with friends? How do you organize the beginning of your week on Sunday night? Each week has a rhythm with regular beginnings and endings. There is also a rhythm to the months of the year. In many early

Building a Community Through Breakfast Club

In my family child care program, we start the day with a healthy breakfast. When I asked parents if they would like to join us while we eat, Breakfast Club was born. My relationships with families and their relationships with each other have blossomed. It is family engagement at its best!

Breakfast Club is a simple concept. I keep some adult-size chairs near the children's table, and parents are warmly encouraged—but never obligated—to join their children during the half hour when breakfast is served. We enjoy different sets of grown-ups every day (including an au pair, family friends, and grandparents). My husband works with me, and we sit with the children to model good eating habits, demonstrate how our daily table rules work, and talk with the children. Sometimes families demonstrate home rules, too. This gives adults an opportunity to share tips with one another and helps children learn that rules can be different in different places.

Adults can eat, too. Help-yourself coffee or tea is available, and often contributed to our program by families. Adults may finish any leftover food after children leave the table. Those who want a full breakfast pay $5—less than a coffee shop latte and bagel. Since this is in my written policies, expectations are clear and generally respected. The major investment is time, less than 30 minutes a day.

The children begin each day surrounded by people who care about them. In this comfortable, family-like setting, good-byes are less stressful. Unlike quick, clingy drop-offs, children walk away first. They might also climb into parents' laps to enjoy extra hugs. Adults can indulge their children because no one is in a hurry. As the children move on to chosen play activities, adults often continue chatting comfortably.

Information is exchanged and relationships are built. During conversations we talk about a range of topics—from the changing weather to the latest sports thrill. We puzzle together over children's behavior or the healthiest ways to discuss the death of a pet. Sometimes parents set up play dates with an ease that only authentic relationships bring.

Everyone's day starts in friendly, relaxed ways. Research shows that the brain opens to its highest level of thinking when people feel supported and valued in a safe, predictable environment. When the children and I begin morning meeting, adults leave ready for work because they feel acknowledged and appreciated by their fellow adults. That's a surprise bonus of Breakfast Club—it helps everyone thrive.

Supporting Dual Language Learners

This warm tradition can be a wonderful opportunity for families from different cultures and who speak different languages to get to know each other. Make an extra effort to invite people who are not sure if they are welcome because of their language differences. Diverse groups may take a little more support from staff to get conversations going, so ask questions you know will interest all the families. Get things started by introducing a few simple greetings or phrases in everyone's language. Ask families to share foods or recipes from home to help all families feel more comfortable.

Adapted from L.A. Manfredi/Petitt, "Building a Community Through Breakfast Club," *Teaching Young Children* 7 (3): 20–21, 2014. www.naeyc.org/tyc/files/tyc/breakfast.pdf.

childhood settings, the program begins in August or September as children join classrooms for the first time or move from one classroom to another. Throughout the year different months are marked by events that connect with families or the larger community. Establishing weekly and monthly rituals can create memories that may last for a lifetime. Long after her child left Jacky's preschool class, one parent shared this memory: "I remember the monthly Friday breakfasts. It was a way to come together as a community, sitting before going to work and having a cup of coffee with other parents. When my sons first went to kindergarten, it was a difficult adjustment as we longed for the community sense we had with all the children and their families. That simple social event of Friday breakfast is still a warm memory."

Young children need predictable schedules for many reasons. For example, knowing what comes next helps them begin to understand the concept of time. In the article "Calendar Time for Young Children: Good Intentions Gone Awry," the authors discuss how calendar time is often used inappropriately because it does not connect to children in a meaningful way (Beneke, Ostrosky, & Katz 2008). They recommend teaching time by using a "picture schedule," making events meaningful by attaching significance to the days, weeks, and months through pictures. You can use this calendar approach to represent the weekly and monthly rituals that you develop for the children you teach.

Weekly Routines Can Become Rituals

Sunday	Monday	Tuesday	Wednesday	Thursday	Friday	Saturday
				1	2	3
4	Happy Face Day 5	6	7	8	9	10
11	12	13	14	15	Music & Dance 16	17
18	19	20	Chapter Book Day 21	22	23	24
25	26	27	28	29	30	31

Days-of-the-Week Rituals

Rituals that welcome children to the beginning, middle, or end of each week help them begin to develop a concept of time. This concept is more easily understood when it is marked with important moments and activities. In "Marking Time: The Significance of Anniversaries," Webber (2011) states, "I wonder if marking these regular events gives us a sense that life has a structure and a rhythm rather than being random, chaotic and unpredictable? Within the familiar structure given to us by anniversaries, perhaps we can tolerate a certain amount of chaos and unpredictability, knowing that we have a number of fixed points ahead in the life of the family or the community." Creating moments—rituals—that children can look forward to, count on, and predict make some of life's unpredictable moments manageable and less scary. When children understand that there is a beginning, middle, and end to days, weeks, and months they are likely to feel safe and secure. "At both a conscious and unconscious level, the child has to feel secure here and now, but at the same time learn that the world out there is not an insurmountable risk, but a place that she can and will learn to manage, learn from, be a part of, and love" (Greenman 2005, 51).

Weekly rituals can mark the beginning, middle, and end of the week, noting the passage of time. How can you mark time for children who attend school on two or three days? It is even more important to give them a welcoming ritual. Even though it may be Tuesday or Wednesday, it is the beginning of their week. Singing a "Good Morning" ritual song to that child on Tuesday so he feels welcome can help him quickly join in the day's activities. In Kaitlyn's program, teachers glue small photos of children on tongue depressors. They have a wall chart with pockets for each child's tongue depressor that, when filled, shows the children who they will see that day. When a child places his tongue depressor in the pocket, he also chooses his special job of the week. One of those jobs is to be the greeter, who gives each child a special greeting no matter which day is his "Monday"!

When Jacky coaches teachers, she suggests that they start by developing a ritual for one or two days of the week and work toward designating something special for each day to mark it as unique. By determining a clear *purpose* for the ritual, choosing *tools* that are meaningful to the ritual and to the children, and *individualizing* the ritual, it is likely that it will meet the needs of the children. Think about something that children will remember and mark each day as something special. Jacky designated Mondays as Happy Face Days to signify that on the first day of the week after the weekend something new and different would start. One week Jacky set out sensory activities in various bins around the room. After the children read and enjoyed a number of books about going to a doctor's office, the next week the children arrived to find a few props for a doctor's office in the dramatic play area. The idea is to set up something that relates to the children's interests and invites them to interact, beginning the week in an exciting, fun manner.

At the first circle time on Monday, Jacky prominently displayed in the classroom a note, a figurine, or something concrete that represented what was special about that day and used it as a sneak peek into the classroom. The children would often find the new item and start asking questions, getting curious about what would be discussed or taught that week. Jacky chose items for different purposes. Maybe it was to highlight a special activity, like making a bean cake. Maybe it was something to help the children remember what they did the previous day that they might want to continue exploring. Or the object provoked the children's interest—a hint of something to come. One week the sneak peek was a dragon puppet sitting with a pretend cake on its lap. The children came to circle time very curious about why the dragon was holding a cake. That week the class began the study of castles, beginning with baking a bean cake that day (Scully, Howell, & Corbey-Scullen 2000). (See p. 63 for more about the bean cake.)

Over time, the opening circle grew into a ritual that Jacky called Talking Time—a time to informally sit together and just talk about the past weekend or anything else the children wanted to talk about, which included bad dreams and flavors of ice cream. It was a warm and inviting way to begin the week together.

Magical Mondays. Javier, a preschool teacher, tells how 3½-year-old Paige would dance into the classroom on Mondays singing, "It's Monday, it's Monday, magical, magical Monday!" Inspired by Paige's chant, Javier filled a zipped canvas bag with what he calls his "Magical Monday" items. The bag holds crowns, wands, glitter, magic wands, and other magical props. He starts Mondays with Paige's Magical Monday chant and then walks around sprinkling glitter to welcome the children. He then places one of the Magical Monday items in an area for the children to use that day.

Good Monday Morning. A positive ritual can welcome everyone back and gather them to start the week. A special activity, chant, or song can

intentionally connect children and make them feel safe and secure as they return to school. For example, every Monday Sophia sings a special Monday "Good Morning" song, such as the one by Natii Wright (www. natiiarts.com), as a welcome-to-the-new-week ritual. At the end of the song, Sophia gives each child a good morning ticket to start the week together. Each ticket is personalized with the child's name and picture and images of a few of that child's favorite things. Sophia has created a special way to bond with children in the beginning of the first day of the week. The tools she uses are both the song and the tangible, individualized good morning ticket. This is a unique ritual in Sophia's classroom, but you can modify it to make it work for the children you teach by identifying your purpose, finding the right tool, and personalizing it to respond to the children you teach so the song and any other tool you use, such as the tickets that Sophia uses, connect with the children's interests and cultures.

Monday Yoga Day. On Mondays every class in Kimberly's center has yoga for all the children and teachers at the center. This is a time when children can breathe deeply, stretch, and connect with one another and their teachers. This Monday yoga class allows children to bond with their teachers at the beginning of the week with a moment of reflection, quiet, and calm.

Chapter Book Wednesdays. Reading chapter books on Wednesdays is a ritual that became a tradition for Ann's preschool class. She makes every Wednesday special by turning out the lights at circle time. She has a special battery-powered lantern that she turns on. The children sit around the lantern for circle time. Ann chooses a chapter book that reflects the children's interests, although she reads other books that she selects based on her interests. To extend children's learning and interests, Ann adds materials to centers that relate to the story. Each week the children look forward to hearing the next chapter and discovering the materials that Ann adds to the classroom.

Friday music, dance, book, or song. An end-of-the-week ritual can be very simple. Mark the passage of time with something that you do only on Friday, such as dance a certain good-bye dance, read a Friday good-bye book, or sing a Friday good-bye song. Cecilia, who teaches 3-year-olds, sings "See You Later, Alligator" with the class to send them on their way each week. You can individualize this ritual for the children you teach by selecting a song that reflects their interests, language, and culture. If you have one or more dual language learners, learn a song or a one-sentence chant in their home language.

Ann's Story

As a pre-K teacher, I look for new and tangible ways to provide fun and challenging activities that link children to each other and to the teachers. Collaboration among educators can serve as a strong basis for this connection. The following example eventually became a tradition in my classroom. It began with a ritual of reading chapter books with the pre-K children I taught. Jacky, who works as a coach in my classroom, introduced me to the book *My Father's Dragon,* by Ruth Stiles Gannett, which was read to Jacky when she was a child. This book contains many elements that can be used to foster children's listening skills, build language skills, and more importantly bring the class together with a common goal—rescuing the baby dragon, the main theme in the book. I created a variety of props to be used with the story, including a map, backpacks like the main character uses, and figures that represent the characters in the book.

This year we used the book as the theme for our fall celebration, BookOWeen, when children dress up as characters from children's books. The children choose their favorite character and create appropriate costumes with their families. Then they participate in our school's annual festival of books. Each year the book I read and how children participate is different. This weekly ritual—reading a chapter book—has been part of the classroom for three years and is now an established tradition in my classroom.

Field Trip or Visitor Fridays. Jacky always ended the week with a field trip, either an in-house field trip or a trip away from the school. In-house field trips are a great and practical way to bring the community to you (the fire department, nature center, doctor; see Reinhard 2014/2015). The routine of having special visitors and field trips became a ritual when Jacky added the intention of making each field trip meaningful to the children in the class. The tool she used was an often nervous puppet who needed lots of information to feel comfortable. Jacky's class also had certain songs that they sang on the bus that were often unique for each new class. Field Trip Fridays became a tradition in Jacky's Dinosaur Classroom for more than 15 years! The week ended with children having an adventure with one another, their teachers, and sometimes their families. This ritual intentionally included opportunities for families and staff to come together the day of the field trip, take part in the brainstorming about where to go and how to plan for the day itself, and work together to have successful field trips. This ritual continued for many years until it became a tradition in Jacky's school. A former student said, "I remember the field trips to the Washington Mystics' game . . . it was my first exposure to women's basketball. The three years I was in your class I looked forward to those trips, and my family eventually got season tickets! We knew the songs to sing and dance to at the game like 'YMCA.' We knew the players' names to cheer for, and we knew when to yell 'DE-FENSE!'"

End-of-the-week poster. To say good-bye to the children each Friday, Andrea creates posters displaying photos taken during the week. She posts them where families can see them when they come to pick up their children. This helps the families feel that they shared the week with Andrea and the children. This ritual, which the children and families look forward to seeing every Friday, connects the families to the class. These same posters can be posted on a classroom blog for those families who do not get to see them at the end of the day.

Rituals throughout the week. Once you have rituals firmly established for the beginning, middle, and end of the week, consider creating a ritual for each day of the week. Think about what is important to the children you teach, to their families, to you, and to your community, and match the rituals you create to what you learn. For example, if you have many families for whom English is a second language, choose a day of the week and play music in that family's language when the families come in the morning. Invite parents to participate and share music that they love with the class. This simple ritual is important because it allows diverse families to participate in the life of the classroom.

Children can help create special daily rituals as well. Listen and pay attention to what children are passionate about. Is it nature, music, or animals? In Kimberly's school, the children are passionate about pets. The school has fish, turtles, and a hedgehog! Thursday is Pet Visit Day. Children spend time with different animals by visiting the classes and areas in the school that have animals and pets. The school even has a pet mascot, one of the teacher's dogs who comes in for Thursday visits as well.

The possibilities are endless. They might include Dance or Story Day Tuesday, Cooking Thursday, or Outdoor Wednesday.

- Tina's school focuses on outdoor curriculum and play time in nature, so she developed a midweek nature hike ritual. Tina and the children collect items from the walk and put them in a nature treasure box to be taken home at the end of the week. The children have a tangible reminder of their week to take home and talk about with their families.

- Kaitlyn's coteacher, Anthony, loves music. Their class has Thursday dance parties, and they share their song lists with the children's families. Both children and adults choose songs for the dance party. This ritual is now an ongoing tradition in this preschool classroom.

- One ritual in Sonia's classroom is Treasure Hunt Friday. She has a basket (the "treasure box") she keeps in the room. Throughout that week at cleanup time, Sonia collects items that children and staff alike are unsure where they belong. On Fridays, she pulls out the basket and the children go on a "treasure hunt" to figure out where the items belong. Each child picks an item and searches throughout the classroom to find the place where it belongs, a perfect end-of-the-week ritual!

Weekly Rituals

There are many ways to create weekly rituals that connect the school community to families at home. Many families are unable to spend time in classrooms, so it is important to create rituals that allow families who cannot be in the classroom to still feel a part of it. Providing rituals like Child of the Week or Taking the School Pet Home allow families to connect with the other children and families in the class.

Child of the Week. For one week, Juanita, who teaches 4-year-olds, celebrates one child as an important member of the class community. At the beginning of the year, she lets the families know when each child will be celebrated so they can plan and be involved in this celebration. If possible, the celebration happens around the child's birthday week. Juanita creates a special poster board for each child. On the poster board she includes information about the child and his family. On Monday of the child's week, he brings in family pictures, a special object to share with others, and a recipe for his favorite food to make. Juanita puts photos on the board, including some when he was a baby, current pictures, and pictures of the family and pets if they are part of the family. Each child also brings his favorite music to share. Every day is marked by something special, including a way to involve the child's family in a way that they choose. Some come in to cook the child's favorite food, like Miguel's mother, who made empanadas with the class. Others come in and read the child's favorite book, play his favorite music, or just spend time in the classroom.

Though it may seem like a long time to wait for children to have their special week, scheduling it around birthdays makes it a bit easier. Some teachers make birthday charts or displays, arranged by months of the year. As children wait for their birthdays, they learn that their special week happens when their birthday appears on the class calendar.

Juanita learned about this ritual at a workshop that Jacky gave on rituals and traditions. The purpose of the ritual is to recognize and learn about each member of the class community. Juanita makes sure that the poster board, music, items from home, or food the children bring reflect the uniqueness of each child. She works with the families to make each child's week special.

Jacky used this ritual with the preschoolers she taught, and over time it became a tradition. When Jacky had dinner at the home of one of her former students, who was 16 at the time, he brought out his special week poster from his time in preschool with Jacky.

Taking the school pet home. Miriam, a teacher at Kimberly's center, has a class pet, Beary, a stuffed animal. Each week Miriam selects a child to take care of Beary for the weekend. She also gives the family a journal and asks them to take photos and write about Beary's adventures with the family on the weekend. The entries in the journal describe how much fun the families have had with Beary, including pictures or stories of experiences, such as reading with Beary at the library, singing songs in the family's home language, and having dinner with the family. The families write in the journal what their child says about Beary's weekend adventures. The families work with their child to create the pages. This gives Miriam a unique insight into each family. When Miriam reads the journal entries to the class, there is often a surprise adventure that makes teachers and children alike laugh out loud.

The child shares the journal when she brings Beary back on Monday, connecting the weekend with her family with the week Beary spends at school. This is an important weekly ritual because children look forward to hearing about Beary's adventures every Monday. They also learn about the child's family and what they do when they are not at the center. Friday is an important day as Beary goes home with a new family. This ritual links the children's school with their home; Beary is the ambassador between the children's two families. Children love sharing Beary with their families and their friends as Beary travels, dines, and visits with a family, and then always comes home to the school community. This ritual gives families an opportunity to share part of their home life with the other children and the teachers. It uses the simple tools of a stuffed animal school pet and a journal, which connect children, families, and teachers.

Some programs have real pets visit children's homes in the same way that Beary visits. In Kimberly's center, Freddi brings her dog in every month. He spends the day being loved, fed, and cared for by the children. They consider him their class pet and look forward to his visits and caring for him.

Monthly Rituals

Some early childhood programs operate year round while others run for a nine-month period, accommodating a wide variety of schedules for children and families. Each program figures out what works best, including how to

Weekend with the Family

It was the best of times; it was the worst of times. . . . .

In the spirit of honesty, I must say my weekend with Amelia, Will and the family started off pretty rough. I was immediately rushed

with Amelia to the dentist to get her teeth cleaned. She was very brave and listened to everything the dentist had to say. Much to my surprise the dentist even gave me a check-up! He told me I need to slow down on the honey intake and brush my teeth twice a day. All in all the trip to the dentist was great.

On Saturday we all drove to the United States Naval Academy to see the Navy football team at their Fan Appreciation Day. I have always been a huge Navy and Notre Dame fan so it was very exciting to meet some of the football players. We got to run around on the football field and jump in two different bounce houses. One was in the shape of a huge aircraft carrier navy ship! Amelia's brother Will went to get a balloon sword and got one for Amelia too. Amelia and I waited in line for a long

What a Director Can Do

Monday Staff Memo

Sharing information and ideas, along with inspiration and humor, is critical to building a school community. It can be challenging to get everyone together for staff meetings or find time to speak individually with every teacher. Directors are always looking for creative ways to share information with everyone in the school, such as a Monday Memo that has details about the upcoming week, inspirational or humorous quotes (especially quotes from teachers), anecdotes, and congratulations for accomplishments. The purpose is to share information, link people together, and inspire staff. What may begin as a simple communication tool often becomes a personal weekly ritual that teachers and administrators alike look forward to.

Monday Morning Memo:

This week Freddi will open every day except Thursday when Kimberly will open. Kimberly will be out on Friday.

Congratulations to Gloria who is engaged! We wish her the best!

Remember to bring in your baby pictures to display in the hall for our Find Your Teacher Contest. We will put up a poster in the hallway and families and teachers will try to figure out which baby picture belongs to which teacher! If you are brave, please bring in an awkward photo from your childhood, which we will display in the Staff Room for teachers to look at and guess who is who!

Parent Teacher Conferences will be held next month so we will give you time to prepare over the next few weeks. Your observations should already be entered but you will have time and coverage to work on putting together the conference reports over the next few weeks. Pod Coordinators will ensure that teachers have planning time to prepare for the conferences by arranging coverage throughout the month. Please let me know if you have any questions.

You can use my office, Freddi's office, or the little conference room to meet with families. Please give Freddi and me a copy of the conference schedule so we know if and when you need one of our offices.

We are excited to announce that Preschool Yoga is starting next Wednesday. We will use all the floaters and myself to make it possible for everyone to participate. The first class will begin at 9:30am, the second class at 10:15am and the third at 11am. Please remind parents to be on time so everyone can enjoy yoga class.

Thank you for your curriculum submissions. Freddi and I read through them, and we are stopping by classrooms to see how the curriculum is going. Thank you for your hard work!

*** *Creativity: Take the obvious, add a cupful of brains, a generous pinch of imagination, a bucketful of courage and daring, stir well and bring to a boil.* ***

Bernard Baruch

celebrate the seasons and months of the year. If a program operates on a school calendar, then September is a month of new beginnings and new classrooms. October is a period of settling in and discovery. November is about thankfulness and spending time with family and friends. December brings holidays for many, with time spent with families and away from school. Highlighting the rhythm of each month is a way of marking time that can help children begin to understand the passage of time. As Cox states, "The good thing about a monthly ritual is that it's regular but also special. There is time for anticipation . . ." (2012, 122). Monthly rituals can become personal and purposeful if you connect the special identity of each month to the abilities, needs, and interests of the children you teach.

Recognize and celebrate each month by using a ritual to welcome and say good-bye to each month. Some teachers write the name of each month on a board at the beginning of each month. They look at how they can embrace each month by celebrating each one as a unique and special time. For example, the month may be special because it is the beginning of the school year. Or it's the month that the ducks are expected to hatch. Maybe the month is acknowledged by celebrating those who have contributed something special or unique to our world. Another way is by working with the children's families to celebrate the holidays that are important to them. (See Chapter 4 for more information.)

At the end of every month, find ways to celebrate what was accomplished that month. Have a family celebration potluck in your classroom each month to connect with the children and their families. Have a monthly art and science show to share with families and other classes in the center all that the children in the class created, discovered, and built during the month. Create a monthly picture slide show or photo album showing what occurred in the class during the month. Not only will families love seeing this, children will love sharing memories of what happened throughout the month. With the children, remember all the special moments when they have been kind and caring. Write them down and celebrate during a special party or "Peace Assembly" (see http://peacefirst.org/digitalactivitycenter/files/rituals_toolkit_10.30.2012_0.pdf). These rituals mark the passing of a month and connect the families and children in a celebration of their successes and achievements.

Pajama Day. One year Kimberly's center celebrated April with a Pajama Day during the Week of the Young Child. Children, teachers, and families loved it and looked forward to it all year. It was so popular that families, children, and teachers asked, wrote letters and emails, and pleaded for regular pajama days. The children and staff liked the relaxed atmosphere of wearing pajamas and spending the day together in their comfy clothes reading books, having campouts, and connecting. What began as a once-a-year event has become a

monthly tradition because it resonated with the children and adults at the center. Now, on the first Monday of every month, children dress in pajamas and spend time with their teachers and one another as they laugh and smile and have pajama day. They sleep in sleeping bags and enjoy one another's company. It is not just a fun monthly event or an excuse to wear pajamas but an experience with special meaning that the children and staff at the school share. Sometimes, they even wear the same pajamas, which happened (see photo) at Kimberly's center.

Creating calendars. Working with children to create monthly calendars can help them connect to each other, to their families, and to their teachers. Creating these calendars can also be an important ritual. A calendar can include a variety of special days, meaningful events, and celebrations such as Chinese New Year, Detective Day, National Teddy Bear Day, National Bike to School Day, or cultural holidays that families celebrate.

■ Ann draws each month on a whiteboard. She writes important events or special activities on the calendar, such as weekly rituals, birthdays, and celebrations. Every month the children add special days to the calendar (see Chapter 4 for additional information). When it is time for a new month, she and the children erase the previous month and draw the new one together. This ritual gives children opportunities to write and to see information shared in more than one language. Ann writes some activities on the calendar in the children's languages. She also selects activities that reflect the interests of the children, teachers, and families in the class.

■ Alejandro and the 4-year-olds he teaches mark special moments on a calendar *after* the events occur. For example, on Wednesday he might post a picture of the children who played soccer that day, or he will paste a leaf from the playground on the day when the children explored the playground and collected leaves. He also places a note on that day that describes what the children were doing. Children sometimes draw their own pictures on the calendar. At the end of the month, he laminates the calendar and posts it on the wall. The children like to show the calendar to their families as they touch, feel, and see what they did that month. This activity also helps children build early literacy skills as they draw or dictate what they did in either their home language or in English as well as reflect on and talk about events that occurred in the past.

Calendars that children help create and that are filled with moments that are meaningful to them result in calendars that belong to the entire class. Research shows that young children do not truly understand the concept of time until the first or second grade (Beneke, Ostrosky, & Katz 2008). While some children can memorize the sequence of the days of the week, they lack a full understanding of what a day actually is. With this in mind, look for meaningful ways to introduce preschoolers to concepts such as *before* and *after* and *later* and *next*. One way to do this is to use a calendar to keep track of important events. Mark the days *before* a visitor is coming, the *next* days when school will be closed, fun events that are scheduled for *later* in the month, or the day *after* a field trip. This approach helps children learn the purpose of calendars and understand how calendars can be useful to them.

Creating monthly calendars can give children a sense of security, letting them know what is going to happen and what has already happened. When children are involved in the creation of calendars, the result can be a meaningful and personal ritual that highlights special memories for teachers, children, and families.

Rituals to Mark Beginnings and Endings

There are many moments in early childhood programs when something is just starting or ending. One instance may be honoring and welcoming a person or pet to the classroom. And then there are times when people or pets leave. Some are expected; others happen suddenly, such as a pet dying. How can you create rituals that mark these beginning and endings?

Welcome song. When Danielle's class got a new pet, all the children gathered around the tank to welcome him to their room. They sang their classroom welcoming song and then worked together to come up with a name. The children used the same ritual Danielle uses to welcome children into the class to welcome their pet!

Death of a class pet or animal. One year a duck passed away after hatching (see p. 57). The children were naturally both curious and upset. Andrew, who at 4 years old was a leader in the classroom, knew what to do to say good-bye to our duck. One ritual that Andrew's class used when a child moved to another state was to make a poster board of the child. They wrote on the board things the children and teacher wanted to remember about the child who was moving, hung it in the room to see, and gathered around holding hands and chanting "We wish you well," which is based on a song by Jack Hartmann. (You can also use the one developed by Becky Bailey—see https://consciousdiscipline.com/resources/songs-and-chants.asp—or develop your own chant with the children.)

Although we did not have a photograph of the duck, Andrew gathered the children in a circle around the incubator. He reminded us to hold hands and chant "We wish you well." Jacky remembers thinking how glad she was that this ritual was already established for children and staff who have moved on and that Andrew suggested using it for the duck. There are many resources that provide guidance about how to work with young children who are grieving for a pet or a person. Think about what ritual might work best for your classroom community (see Davis 2001 and NAEYC 2009b).

Departure of a teacher or child. There are times when people leave both for reasons that are expected as well as reasons that we are unprepared for such as death. What rituals you choose to use to acknowledge these times depend to a large extent on the children and their families, and the values of the program where you teach. You will need to consider many factors (see Davis 2001 and NAEYC 2009b). One ritual 4-year-old Kaleb's class has for a child who moves is to create a poster of that child, using the "I Wish You Well" ritual from Becky Bailey's *Creating a School Family* (2011) that the children say for a couple weeks after the child has left.

❖　❖　❖　❖　❖　❖

Weekly and monthly rituals build connections, a sense of community, and a sense of security. Teachers develop rituals that reflect the interests and needs of the children they teach, creating a safe environment where children are able to learn and develop. Weekly rituals mark the beginning, middle, and end of the school week and can connect family life and school life. Rituals such as sending home the class pet allows families to participate even if they cannot come in to the classroom. Other rituals, such as Yoga Mondays or Pajama Days, allow children and teachers to connect. Rituals and traditions are important for everyone—children, families, and teachers.

In the Next Chapter

What are yearly rituals and traditions and how can you create them? Chapter 4 outlines how to develop annual, seasonal, and holiday traditions that are unique and special for the children you teach. The chapter will also explain the importance of marking milestones with children and families.

Reflections

- What rituals do you use to mark the days of the week for the children you teach?

- What routines and rituals do you plan that form the structure of the week? How can you create a special ritual to mark one or more days of the week?

- How do you help children mark the passage of time? Select one or two ideas in this chapter with the goal of adding a special celebration for each month that may help children recognize the passage of each month.

4

Creating Yearly Traditions

> David runs into his preschool classroom early in the morning and
> calls out, "Have they hatched yet? Have they hatched yet?" Jacky,
> his teacher, says, "Come over to the incubator. I think I see a mark on
> the egg where one might be pecking out!" Soon other children and
> families, from both current and past classes, arrive to watch the ducks
> hatching, an annual tradition in this classroom.

Jacky began incubating chicken and duck eggs as a celebration of spring; she
had fond memories of her first grade teacher incubating chicken eggs and
watching them hatch. She originally thought it would be a one-time event.
However, because the children were so interested in and excited about the
activity, she decided to do it every spring. After children left Jacky's school their
families continued to ask when the hatching might happen so they could bring
their children back to see the baby chickens or ducks. This event became a
tradition that many children and families remembered, and Jacky has coached
teachers who have decided to incorporate this tradition in their classrooms.

   In Chapter 1 traditions were defined as "significant events that have a special
history and meaning and that occur year in and year out. Traditions are a part
of the history; they reinvigorate the culture and symbolize it to insiders and
outsiders alike. . . . When people have traditions that they value and appreciate,
it gives them a foundation to weather challenges, difficulties, and change" (Deal
& Peterson 1999, 33). The focus of this chapter is on how teachers can do the
following:

- Develop unique traditions that are developmentally appropriate (individually, age, and culturally appropriate) and based on the interests of children, teachers, and staff
- Use traditions to connect staff
- Develop annual celebrations that can become traditions
- Turn milestones into traditions
- Transform seasonal events into traditions
- Find a place for cultural and religious holidays

Rituals and traditions can go hand in hand, or each may stand alone. Rituals reinforce traditions; traditions create the history of a class or program. Rituals can arise spontaneously or be planned intentionally for many reasons, including to make occasions meaningful to children, ease transitions, and build connections. Traditions, on the other hand, reflect history and happen at expected times. They can be changed and adjusted, yet still reflect the original intentions and often the people who have established them. They may be cultural, related to holidays, or specific to a family, a class, a group, or a program. There may be rituals embedded in traditions: For example, the I Love You Dinner tradition contained many rituals, such as the creation of an invitation by the children, the same menu and time of year, and the song the children sang. All of these contributed to a tradition that lasted for years.

In early childhood programs, traditions are reflective of the lives, histories, or experiences and cultures of the people who work there. Teachers and administrators stay long after children and their families leave. Establishing traditions that reflect the values, intentions, culture, and experiences of staff, children, and families creates something valuable for everyone.

Both Jacky's and Kimberly's programs have significant traditions developed by individual classes or by the programs. For example, on the first Saturday in May each year, Jacky's center holds a May Fair complete with games, food, and other events. Although the tradition of the May Fair is constant, some aspects might change each year. For example, the families that help plan the event might decide one year to have Ethiopian food or to ask a reggae group to perform. What stays the same is that food and music are part of each May Fair. What changes are the details, which are decided by the families who plan the event each year.

Gail, one of the teachers in Kimberly's center, always celebrates Grandparents Month in December. Another teacher has a summer tradition. Her class grows a garden and sells the food they grow in a "café." Some traditions are classroom based and others, like the May Fair, are supported and celebrated by the whole program.

Having traditions like these help define a class or a program. They create a rhythm to the year that is familiar and predictable, engage families and teachers in planning each event, and offer opportunities for changing the event so it reflects the families, children, and teachers who are in the class or program that year. Repeating these traditions over time is one way that a class or program defines itself and fosters a classroom or program community and identity. Some traditions remain long after the teacher leaves because they are ingrained in the program.

One tradition that Jacky's Dinosaur Classroom instituted was to write a play developed by the children (see Corbey-Scullen & Howell 1997). This tradition evolved over time as children and families suggested new ideas that were incorporated. The I Love You Dinner tradition contained rituals within it and also changed over the years. The menu and song ("Skinnamarink") remained constant, yet some of the singing rituals changed. For example, one year the dinner featured a big sing-along with the children and families singing together instead of only the children singing. Although the traditional celebration was always held in February, it evolved over time with input from the children, teachers, families, and community.

Traditions in early childhood classrooms and programs come in many forms. They can be part of celebrations, holidays, cultural events, or seasonal happenings, or they may recognize children's milestones and development. They often reflect and define the community in early childhood settings.

Unique Celebrations Based on the Interests of Children, Teachers, or Families

As you think about establishing a tradition, keep in mind the topics and events that children are interested in and the traditions that their families celebrate. You can spark children's interests when you share with children and their families traditions that are important to you or to them. Giving families opportunities to share their traditions with the other children also fosters a sense of community. Introducing the children to a tradition that is important to you or to the families gives children an opportunity to explore new ideas. You can engage children's interests in a tradition by setting up the classroom environment with learning center materials, books, and other items related to the topic of that tradition.

For example, if you are an avid gardener and you have developed a spring tradition of exploring the topic of gardening, you might involve families by asking them to help you select plants to place in appropriate areas of the classroom. You might also add dirt, shovels, and "bugs" in the sensory table. The new plants in the classroom may intrigue children, as will the opportunity to dig in the dirt. They may ask questions about plants, such as "Why are the plants by the window?" and "Can I water the plants?" and "Why can't we all water the plants?" The materials in the classroom will spark children's curiosity about gardening. Adding inviting materials that relate to a tradition gives children an opportunity to expand their understanding and gain information related to the tradition. These classroom "invitations" allow children to explore ideas and connections and then make them their own (Curtis 2004).

Keen writes,

> Official holidays and national celebrations punctuate our time, stop the flux of our days, and remind us to pay attention to the rhythms and seasons of our lives. . . . But just beneath the surface of our official holidays, there lies a world of private celebrations and ritual occasions, special events in the lives of families and friends. . . . Over my desk I have a quotation from the film *A Thousand Clowns* to remind me of what is important: "You have got to own your days and name them, each one of them, every one of them, or else the years go right by and none of them belongs to you." When I can keep my wits about me, I create my own calendar and mark special holidays. (1994, 267–68)

There are many ways to create yearly celebrations that may become traditions in your classroom or program. One of them is to create a unique calendar with special events. In the calendar shown on page 61, there are examples of days that can be part of the curriculum and that may become traditions. One place to begin is to select one or two monthly events and talk with the children about the events. Use a resource like Chase's Calendar of Events (see Resources on p. 103) to find unusual holidays, celebrations, national and international special occasions, and events from Creativity Month to Banana Pudding Lovers Month. Celebrations and special days can also grow from family traditions. One mother in Jacky's preschool class loved doing crossword puzzles. She designed a life-size puzzle on a large sheet of paper that was simple enough for 3- and 4-year-olds. It incorporated the children's names and familiar words they would recognize. It was so popular that even after this

November

Sunday	Monday	Tuesday	Wednesday	Thursday	Friday	Saturday
						1
2	Sandwich Day 3	4	5	Sax Day 6	7	Sweet potato 8 Day
9	10	Veteran's Day 11	12	World Kindness Day 13	14	Recycle Day 15
16	Home Made 17 Bread Day	18	19	Universal 20 Children's Day	21	22
Mother Goose 23 Day	24	25	Puzzle Day 26	27	28	29

family left the program, Jacky continued to put this event on the calendar. A tradition was born!

When you find a celebration that engages the interests of the children or their families, you add an element of playfulness and connect with children and families to foster the development of a classroom community. These times might become meaningful traditions. Here are a few more examples.

Baking Bread Day. Latisha cooked and baked with her mother, and she wanted to continue this tradition with the preschool children she teaches. Every November 17, otherwise known as Homemade Bread Day, she bakes bread with the children in her class. It often sparks conversations with the children about baking bread and what it means to their teacher. When this happens, Latisha tells the children about baking bread with her mother. What started as a special day has become a yearly tradition on November 17. Every year she tweaks the tradition to reflect the class by using bread recipes from the children's families. Sharing cooking and baking experiences can be wonderful for young children (Colker 2005; Colker & Simon 2014). One ritual that Latisha has added to this tradition is to read or tell the story of the Little Red Hen.

Latisha and the children then bake loaves of bread to share with the children in other classrooms and with people who work at their early childhood setting. The whole school is filled with the smell of the bread baking. Everyone looks forward to the delivery of a loaf of bread by the children in Latisha's class.

Ideas for creating celebrations that are meaningful to you, the children you teach, and their families can come from many sources. Latisha's came from her experience of baking with her mom. Consider the prompts in the box "Reflections About Creating Rituals and Traditions" (see p. 87) as prompts and inspiration to create ideas based on your personal experiences.

Detective Day. The classroom calendar can be filled with unique days to celebrate as a source of traditions to draw a classroom together. For example, Jacky is a fan of mysteries. She read many mysteries to children over the years. Some of the children's favorites were the books in the Nate the Great detective series. One year she decided to celebrate the birthday of Sir Arthur Conan Doyle, the author of books about the great detective Sherlock Holmes. Jacky declared his birthday (May 22) Detective Day. A week before Detective Day, Jacky sent a note home to families to tell them about Detective Day and, with suggestions, to ask them to make detective costumes for their children. The teachers and children alike came dressed in detective disguises on the designated day. Jacky devised a mystery for the children to solve, with clues everywhere. That day, the children went to "detective school" and earned their own detective license. All day the children worked to solve the mystery, including interviewing sources and suspects, and going back to their "office" to discuss the clues. By the end of the day, the mystery of a missing clock was solved: The office assistant had borrowed it, and she forgot to leave a note! This celebration was so popular that Jacky decided to put Detective Day on the calendar the next year and every year after that. This special tradition incorporates a wide variety of learning opportunities and is a project the whole class can work on together.

Rosa Parks Day. Ideas for traditions may come from events centered on historical or cultural figures, particularly if the events celebrate individuals who are meaningful to the teachers, children, and families and reflect shared program values. For example, one child in Tina's classroom went with her family to an event honoring Rosa Parks. When she came to school the next day, she brought in a book about the life of Rosa Parks. Because of an individual child's experience and the response by the class to the book about Rosa Parks, Tina decided to celebrate Rosa Parks's birthday on February 4. One child's interest sparked that of the other children in the class. Tina supported that interest by finding out more about Rosa Parks and sharing information with the children in a meaningful way. Over time, this grew into a yearly celebration in Tina's class.

Depending on the interests, cultures, and languages of the children and families and the values of the program where you teach, you may want to celebrate historical, cultural, and social justice events with the children and their families.

Bean Cake. An idea that Jacky used during short winter days, based on a coteacher's family experience, was baking and eating a bean cake (Scully, Howell, & Corbey-Scullen 2000). The preschoolers baked a cake that had a bean hidden in it. While eating a piece of the cake, they looked for the large lima bean baked inside. Whoever found the bean was crowned king or queen for the day. Jacky followed the children's lead to develop other ideas inspired by the bean cake. One year this included a knighting ceremony; another year the queen chose an emblem for that year's banner. One group of children researched and designed a castle, which they made out of cardboard. They chose different roles to play in the castle and created costumes for each role. One year the queen decided she needed many royal sisters, and they were all co-queens! A classroom kingdom emerged from this

single bean cake yearly tradition. Each year, the king or queen, along with the children in the class, decided what to do. Sometimes it was similar to what the children did the previous year; other times it was quite different. The bean cake tradition is the same; the way the children celebrate it might change from year to year. This tradition, with activities that the children designed, developed a sense of community and offered numerous learning opportunities as the children learned about medieval times and the construction of a classroom castle!

Wacky Days. There are also yearly celebrations that are often referred to as Wacky Days (see Resources on p. 103 for ideas), such as National Hello Day, National Ice Cream Sundae Day, or National Panda Day. Many teachers celebrate these fun days as a way to make the class a special place to be. In Sonia's classroom, she and her teaching team each choose one day each month to try out a unique celebration. One is Our Favorite Movies, an Academy Awards-like celebration in February. She created it based on discussions with the children about the movies and videos they watch. The children learned about the different aspects of creating a movie or video, from being a director to writing the script to acting it out. Each year the children nominate five of their favorite movies, and they watch them together. Then they vote on categories they have created. Finally, they have an awards celebration with voting being done by the "Academy," which of course are the children in the classroom! The children then dress as characters from the movies, or as the director, writer, musician, and so on. Families are invited to attend as the audience. She says that it brings the community of children together for an enjoyable learning activity during a time that is often dreary and cold in their area.

Test your own ideas by developing a celebration that relates to your interests or to the interests of the children or greater community. Eventually, this celebration could become a tradition, one that children and families will look forward to joining. Before children joined one of Jacky's classes, they knew about the traditions that Jacky had developed, which included the I Love You Dinner, hatching ducks or chickens, and Bean Cake Day. At Kimberly's center, they know that the Week of the Young Child is a special weeklong tradition (see the box "Week of the Young Child Festivities" on p. 68).

Using Traditions to Connect Staff

Traditions can also foster connections among staff. Teachers and administrators in an early childhood setting work long hard hours, and it can be a challenge to find time to connect with one another. The priority is always the children. However, holding events that help staff members bond is crucial because it creates a school community of caregivers and educators who work together. Many teachers and staff continue to work together for many years; most children and their families leave after a few years. In addition to staff development days that focus on CPR, first aid, regulations, and curriculum, Kimberly's center holds a yearly staff development day that encourages camaraderie using inventive, fun games with teams. Every year, Kimberly creates a new game for the staff to participate in, from an art scavenger hunt in a local mall (see the box "Process Art Scavenger Hunt") to a race in which

Process Art Scavenger Hunt

This is your mission: You must work as a team to find as many items as possible on the list below. Your team *must stay together* for the duration of the scavenger hunt. Every item must be usable in a classroom. Each team will receive $25. The team that returns with the most items on the list will receive a special prize. You can use any means that you like to complete your assigned task, but you must obtain items from at least 11 places. Be as creative as you like (the more creativity the better). We will meet at La Sandia for debriefing and lunch at 12:30 p.m.

All teams *must* participate! This is a fun adventure for you get to know your colleagues and to work together. Enjoy!

Your mission over the next 2.5 hours:

_____ One item that is purple

_____ Two items that can be used to create a structure over two feet tall

_____ Three items that can be used to create NEW process art classroom projects

_____ Four messy tactile items

_____ Five items that will make different sounds when struck

_____ Six items found in nature

_____ Seven items of different shape and size

_____ Eight containers that make different sounds when filled up

_____ Nine items that can be used in a collage

_____ Ten different items can be used to paint with

teachers are divided into teams to figure out clues and solve puzzles that they find in different locations throughout the community (see the box "The Amazing Race" on p. 66). The Amazing Race teams need to work together to get to their destinations. They might have to roam a toy store, complete a puzzle in the library, or recite a poem in a local coffee shop.

Annual Celebrations

Annual celebrations and festivals that include all the children, families, and staff can become meaningful traditions. Celebrating the Week of the Young Child is a tradition at Kimberly's center. Teachers form a committee to plan each day's themes and develop activities that reflect what is special and interesting to them and the children at the center (spending time outside so children can enjoy nature, honoring the Olympics and sports, exploring art

The Amazing Race

For the Amazing Race, each team receives a clue that leads it to a location in the community (a bookstore, coffee shop, toy store, library, hardware store, or ballet studio). Each team starts in a different place so no two teams go to the same place at the same time. Once the team figures out the clue and arrives at the location, members are given an activity to complete in order to receive their next clue. They may have to complete a jigsaw puzzle together, follow instructions to create a LEGO structure, memorize a poem and recite it all together, or work to create a flower like the sample provided. The clues are provided by the store owners so the teachers have opportunities to get to know the community members. They also determine when the activity is completed successfully and the team has earned its next clue. The team then has to solve the next clue and so forth until it eventually completes the race and returns to the school as winners. What a great way to work together, see the community, solve problems, and have fun outside of school!

Below are examples of the clues:

Amazing Race Clues

Each team is given the first clue at school. Each team receives a different clue that leads to a different site. The teams can use each other, people in the community, their cell phones, or any other resource to research and figure out the meaning of each clue.

Clues: It has spines but no bones. It can whisper or yell but has no voice.

Answer: Bookstore

Clues: Call ahead or go online to reserve one of the things I have. I am one of the only things that is still free these days. I am holding on and waiting for you.

Answer: Library

Clues: I am not a swan but lovely despite the sprains and strains. Just ask Angelina.

Answer: Ballet studio

Clues: People say it is easy but it isn't. Read, Squish, Monopolize, Trivialize, Dress Up, and Enjoy.

Answer: A local toy store

What would work in your community? Alter these ideas so they will work with places in your neighborhood.

These Amazing Race Activities

These are sample Amazing Race activities that teams have completed at a local bookstore, library, coffee shop, and other locations. Teams work together and often discover a colleague's strength outside of the school and outside of her role in school.

- Choose to finish either two 48-piece puzzles or one 100-piece puzzle. Puzzles must be successfully completed and shown to receive the next clue.

- Search this toy store and find a toy you would be excited to use in a classroom. Then take the enclosed lesson plan and fill it out, basing the entire lesson plan (music, art, circle time, etc.) around the toy your team has chosen. Present the lesson plan to the cashier to be reviewed. The cashier will hand you the next clue if he or she is satisfied.

- Open the box of LEGOs. Follow the instructions exactly and make one vehicle (your team may choose which one) according to the instructions. You must present the vehicle to the cashier for approval. If it is correct, your team will receive your next clue. Please disassemble your vehicle before you leave and put the pieces back in box. You do not want to make it too easy for the next team so make sure to take the LEGOs apart and put them back in the box.

and science, etc.). They organize the week accordingly. Each day is different. Sometimes the activities give children and teachers the opportunity to dress up and have a new adventure. Information about the week is distributed to families so they can prepare for each day's theme (Messy Day, Pajama Day, Wacky Day) and mark their calendars for a huge party at the end of the week for families, teachers, and children alike. The party reflects what children are most excited about (dancing to music, having a petting zoo, etc.). This event started as a simple week with a few unique events and has become a week that families and teachers alike look forward to throughout the entire year. The weeklong activities are a big part of the center's sense of identity. The center is known throughout the community as having a unique approach to the Week of the Young Child.

School-wide celebrations can also be a fall festival, a thankful lunch, or a spring party. Start small with an event that is meaningful to your program so the tradition will carry on and become an integral part of your program.

Week of the Young Child Festivities

During the week of April 15–20, we will be celebrating the Week of the Young Child, which is sponsored by the National Association for the Education of Young Children (NAEYC). This week honors young children and the professionals who teach them. We will be planning special activities and experiences every day, culminating in our Spring Party on Friday during which we will have a petting zoo! We hope each class will spend a great deal of time outside taking a nature hike or discovering new animals, plants, and life in the great outdoors.

Monday, 4/15—Goofy Day
(Be silly, goofy, and your true quirky self!)
Let your child embrace his or her kooky self (mismatched socks, backwards shirts, crazy hair/hat, etc.)! Dress the goofiest way possible. **Please bring in lunch.** We plan to have a picnic lunch outside (inside if the weather is bad) to really mix things up and make the day special.

Tuesday, 4/16—Sports Day
(Dress in sports gear that represents your favorite player or team)
We will play sports outside, including soccer, football, basketball, golf, tee ball, and more. We will race and run and play outside all day long. If you have sports equipment that you would be willing to share, please bring it in on Monday.

Wednesday, 4/17—Science and Nature Day
(Dress in clothes to go outside and explore)
Children will spend the day outside, playing on the playground and enjoying the great outdoors. Some classes will go on hikes on the nature trail or to the fishpond. We will dig in the dirt, look at bugs, and collect leaves and acorns.

Thursday, 4/18—Character Day
(Dress as your favorite children's book character and bring in the book to share with the class.)
We will have a wonderful day reading our favorite stories from the children's books that you bring in to share.

Friday, 4/19—Animal Day
(Dress as your favorite animal or a safari/zoo keeper)
We will learn about different animals this day, open up a veterinary clinic in the classroom dramatic play area, and have a real petting zoo visit us in the afternoon for hands-on animal learning! Feel free to bring your child's favorite stuffed animal for nap time and playing.

Spring Party and Petting Zoo at 4:00 p.m.! See you there!

Teacher Addendum for Week of the Young Child

This will be a busy week filled with fun and learning.

Monday—Remember to dress wacky on Goofy Day! Children will dress up as well; make sure to have a few fun items, including hair bands and clips for wacky hairdos, available for anyone who forgot to dress up and wants to. Each pod/class can decide how to be wacky based on what you think the children will enjoy. Let things be as wacky as the children are comfortable with. I have asked families to bring in lunch so we can have a picnic inside or outside. I bought silly straws for all the children to use and take home.

Tuesday—For Sports Day, children will come dressed in sports hats and their favorite team's clothes. Feel free to do the same. Families may bring in sporting equipment. We can hold foot races, use our balance beam, make an obstacle course outside, set up "lawn bowling," and so on. We have balls and equipment that you can use. Yoga will occur as usual.

Wednesday—On Science and Nature Day, take the children on a walk to the fishpond or on the nature trail. Collect leaves, rocks, acorns, and other natural items. Look at bugs with magnifying glasses and dig in the dirt to look for worms. Put natural materials in the water table or take buckets of water outside for the children to paint with or play in since the weather should be nice. Children will come dressed to go outside and get messy.

Thursday—This is Character Day. To embrace the day we are encouraging children to dress as characters from their favorite stories. Their families may bring in books that you can read to the class or invite family members to do so. If the children express interest in doing so, help them make castles (or maybe dragons).

Friday—This is Animal Day, so set up a veterinary clinic, zoo, or teddy bear picnic/tea party in the dramatic play area. The Spring Party will feature a petting zoo at 4:00 pm. We will serve light refreshments and allow families and children to play with the animals until 5:30 pm and then play on the playground until the school closes.

Have a great time during this fun week!

Milestone Traditions

Preschoolers mark many milestones during their years in early childhood settings. These milestones might include the following:

- New beginnings: starting school for the first time, children or teachers beginning a new year, the arrival of a new baby sibling or a new pet
- Endings: end of the school year, children or teachers moving or leaving, loss of a loved one or pet
- Birthdays and anniversaries: if supported by your program, this might include children's birthdays or special dates like the first day of spring or the birthday of a class pet
- Developmental changes: losing a tooth, getting taller, getting glasses, peddling a bike, learning to pump on a swing

New Beginnings

In addition to the daily and weekly rituals described in Chapter 2, new beginnings are a regular part of the lives of young children. One of the most important to children and families is when children start school for the first time or when they move to a new classroom.

Send letters to children. Shavonne, who teaches 3-year-olds, writes letters to the children before their first day in the classroom. The welcome letter tells each child, "I am waiting to meet you. You will have a special cubby with a special sticker where you can store your things from home." Shavonne includes a photo of the classroom and the teachers and a little token to keep or to bring on the first day of school. Because her class is called the Dolphins, the token is often related to the sea, like one of the shells she collects over the summer, or a little figure of a dolphin. Because these letters help the children and families feel comfortable about their new classroom, this is now a tradition that Shavonne follows at the start of the year and before a new child enrolls in the class. This tradition has the elements of a ritual (see p. 20): It is *intentional*— it is used to welcome children into the classroom, it uses *tools*—sending a letter and a photo of the classroom, and a little token to each child, and it is

individualized—it reflects Shavonne and the classroom. Many families tell Shavonne how excited their child felt to receive a welcoming letter in the mail!

Calm children's worries. Kaitlyn, who has many puppets in her classroom, uses a Wemberly puppet similar to the mouse in *Wemberly Worried*, by Kevin Henkes. Her mouse starts school on the first day with the children and has many worries about how things will be. During the first weeks as children adjust to being in a new classroom, Kaitlyn uses Wemberly to model ways children can cope with all the new things. Wemberly waves good-bye at the good-bye window, she cries for her mother sometimes and needs soothing, and when she is looking for a new friend she writes letters to each child. All of the children help Wemberly to adjust by hugging her, helping her draw pictures for her mom, and singing her the comforting song that the class has selected that year. Children whose siblings attended Kaitlyn's class previously look forward to meeting Wemberly, a tradition that helps them transition to their new class.

Beginnings are important in establishing community. In "Pillars of Security," Jim Greenman (1990a) speaks about creating a sense of place that lets children know they belong. What tradition could you develop that lets children know at the beginning of the year that they belong to the class?

Endings

In early childhood settings children experience many endings, those that are expected and those that are unexpected and sometimes tragic. Children or teachers may move to a new school or classroom for many reasons, including the school year ending. Then there are losses that occur due to serious illness or the death of a classroom pet, child, family member, or teacher in the classroom. Even a positive change, such as replacing new furniture or equipment, can feel like a loss to some children. When coping with loss, classroom traditions can offer significant support to children, families, and teachers.

End of the school year. Leaving the class at the end of the year is often marked with a meaningful ceremony or event that families attend. This tradition is a perfect time for creating rituals of remembrance and marking the passage of an important time in young children's lives. As you create this tradition, with input from children and families, think about how to individualize the occasion.

End-of-the-year celebrations represent both the ending of something and the anticipation of a new stage in a child's life. Juanita marks the occasion by turning over the classroom rocking boat to the side with steps, decorating it, and having the children walk "over the bridge" to the new school (see the article "Developmentally Appropriate Practice and Preschool Graduation" [Taharally & La Fontaine 2007]. When choosing the best way to celebrate, take into account what is developmentally appropriate, the culture and languages of the families, and the values of the community and the program.

Jacky established a tradition of involving alumni children and families. She chose a date (usually in May), and invited the children and families who had moved on to kindergarten to attend an afternoon event. She sent out invitations well in advance to maximize participation. The alumni sat in chairs in the front of the room; they brought items and ideas to share from their kindergarten experience. Meanwhile, the children in Jacky's Dinosaur Classroom prepared a list of questions for the visitors and created a special snack for them. Because Jacky's class was mixed age, many of the current children remembered their classmates who had moved on to a new school.

The current Dinosaurs asked the former Dinosaurs questions. Their answers provided a unique insight into the kindergarten experience. It was always a special day for all—with the opportunity to connect with children and families and to witness the changes in the kindergartners. The looks on the former Dinosaurs' faces were very serious as they listened to and answered each question. This tradition lasted many years and was a memorable experience for all. It helped children who were transitioning from preschool to kindergarten understand what to expect through the shared experiences of a former friend or classmate.

A growing-up party. In Imani's class celebration, which he calls a Growing-Up Party, the children participate in creating a book of their milestones that has photos, drawings, and words from throughout the year. The book includes photographs of many of the children's firsts, like pumping on a swing or tying a shoe, maybe a video clip of a child riding a small two-wheel bicycle, the song the class wrote about the field trip to the basketball game that year, as well as other precious memories. Because Imani documents these things all year, he can create a book for each child to give to their families as well as use the documentation to make a slide presentation at the Growing-Up Party. At the celebration, everyone spends time laughing, talking, and sharing memories from the past year. This event is now a tradition in Imani's class. Each celebration reflects the children in the class and the important milestones from that school year.

Birthdays and Anniversaries

Depending on families' religious and cultural practices and a program's policies, some teachers celebrate children's birthdays. Some celebrate other milestone anniversaries, such as the date their program opened. For example, Kimberly's staff celebrated their program's twentieth anniversary with a huge celebration at a park, inviting all former staff and families to return and spend time playing together, eating, and simply reconnecting.

Each program will have its own perspective on what is appropriate for celebrations. As with holiday celebrations, it is important to work with teachers and families to create celebrations that are developmentally appropriate and culturally sensitive. The resource list beginning on page 103 includes information to consider as you begin to develop rituals and traditions around birthdays and other celebrations.

Birthdays. Sarai remembers her childhood birthday celebrations that reflected her Indian heritage. On her birthday she dressed in colorful, new clothing, and instead of a birthday cake she shared a bag of sweets with her classmates. Sarai's fond childhood memories prompted her to develop birthday

Rituals and Traditions

traditions for the children she teaches. She created special birthday hats out of colorful materials with unusual designs. The birthday child selects one of the hats to wear all day so everyone knows it is his or her birthday. She added colorful birthday vests for children who do not want to wear a hat. The birthday child sits in a decorated chair, and the children sing a song they developed and wrote with Sarai, based on the Beatles' song "Birthday."

School anniversary. Nicole works in an early childhood setting that has nine classrooms serving children from birth through preschool. In March of every year the school has a special celebration marking the day the school first opened. Happy Birthday to Our School day is celebrated with cake, decorations, music, and dancing. The children, teachers, and families decorate the gathering room with pictures of children, families, and teachers who have been part of the school. Many alumni families return to attend the event. As part of this celebration, current and alumni families launched a fundraising program that gives families the opportunity to make a donation in the name of their child or to donate something to their child's classroom, such as their child's favorite book. This event brings the present and past school community together to mark a milestone with a tradition that is important to that school community.

Developmental Changes

Preschoolers experience many firsts that are worth celebrating and sharing. Sometimes teachers have the privilege to witness these developmental changes. Creating traditions that mark developmental milestones is an opportunity to make them a special memory for a child and the family and to connect children, families, and teachers.

Watch us grow. Although some early childhood teachers measure a child's height at the beginning of the year and at other points in the year, Cliff, who teaches preschoolers, expands this concept to include helping children slow down and notice the changes in their bodies. One year the class measured how long their arms had grown! Cliff puts four "See How Much We've Grown" dates on the calendar to measure children throughout the year. On those four days, the class sings "I Wonder If I'm Growing" by Raffi. Cliff takes a picture of each child next to his growth chart and keeps it in a book he calls, "We Are the Panthers (his classroom's name)—Watch Us Grow!" Children like to sit and look at the documentation he has created that shows all the ways children have grown and changed throughout the year. At the end of the year, he removes the pages and puts them into separate books for each child to take home to her family. Cliff has completed more than 12 annual books.

There are a number of developmental changes that you could use to create memorable traditions. Look for the ones that resonate with the classroom community, such as documenting when children learn to kick a ball, skip, hop, climb up the slide on their own, or write their names. Be sure to watch for appropriate milestones for children who have physical challenges. For example, if Katie is learning to use a spoon by herself, celebrate when she accomplishes this.

Seasonal Changes

Rachel Carson says,

> Those who contemplate the beauty of the earth find reserves of strength that will endure as long as life lasts. There is symbolic as well as actual beauty in the migration of the birds, the ebb and flow of the tides, the folded bud ready for the spring. There is something infinitely healing in the repeated refrains of nature—the assurance that dawn comes after night, and spring after winter. (1965, 100–101)

Marking seasonal changes in a classroom can be as simple as recognizing different birds at the feeder or noticing that the leaves on your adopted tree have changed color. What traditions might you want to create to mark changes in the seasons? Some changes in your area may be subtle, but noticing something like the days growing shorter or longer can be easy to track. The vignette at the beginning of this chapter describes a seasonal activity of hatching chickens or ducks. It was one way of marking the beginning of spring that was inspired by that teacher's childhood memory.

What are some seasonal changes you might want to help the children notice and then celebrate? Here are some thoughts on each:

Fall: A time of harvest and gathering; the hours of daylight decrease, and it may start to become colder. There are many cultural holidays revolving around our ancestors, like Día de los Muertos, Day of the Dead, in which families and loved ones come together to remember those who have died.

Winter: A quiet time of rest, darkness, and regeneration; many cultures and religions celebrate festivals of light near the shortest day (the day with the least amount of sunlight), which is in winter. Rosalie's preschool class is located in a part of the country where they get plenty of snow each winter. They have an annual tradition they call Welcoming Winter!, which involves welcoming winter rituals the day they all notice the first snowflakes.

Spring: A time of awakening, renewal, and possibility; many cultures celebrate the promise of spring and the changes it will bring. Some programs have traditions of planting flowers in the spring or having an annual picnic that celebrates the change of the season.

Summer: A time of heat, celebration, and abundance; the number of daylight hours reaches its peak (the longest day), and many families take children on a vacation.

Changes in seasons offer inspiration for creating seasonal traditions. Paying attention to the seasonal changes in your geographical area will influence the choices you make. As with holidays, understanding the children's cultural backgrounds will help you plan appropriate seasonal traditions.

Winter. As mentioned earlier, Rosalie's preschool class is located in a place that has snowy winters. As part of their Welcoming Winter tradition, Rosalie rings chimes and plays "Winter" from Vivaldi's *Four Seasons*. Then she reads *The Snowy Day*, by Ezra Jack Keats, to the children. The children begin a traditional class book about winter that captures winter events they like to do together, such as go sledding, have an outdoor winter picnic, and make bird feeders. Each idea is a lovely way to welcome winter.

Wintertime Wonderland

In her workshop at the Virginia Association for Early Childhood Education (VAECE) Conference in 2013, Bev Bos shared two traditions that she created for winter in California. After the holiday, the families who have Christmas trees take them to Bev's school and put them on the playground. The teachers and families create a mini-forest with the trees, which the children use to play in and explore. Because the school is in Sacramento and snow is rare except in the mountains, Bev also borrows a snow-making machine from one of the local ski lodges to blow snow into the outdoor area. These two traditions are a way to mark wintertime in a community that does not typically have cold winters.

Seasonal food. Many teachers plan cooking activities to mark seasonal changes. Within walking distance to Andrea's pre-K program is a farmer's market. Four times a year (once each season), Andrea takes the children to the market and purchases seasonal food. Then the class spends the next week doing lots of cooking, taste testing, and sharing recipes that families send in that use the seasonal foods the class purchased. She marks this time on her calendar every year, and the children and families alike look forward to this event. Every year it is a bit different because the children choose different foods and the families send in different recipes.

Gardening. Many programs have small gardens in which children and teachers grow flowers, herbs, and even fruit and vegetables. Children plant seeds, tend to the soil and weeds, water the garden, and watch the flowers or vegetables grow throughout the spring or summer. This is a hands-on way to celebrate the seasons and the changes that occur in nature. In Kimberly's center, families are invited every spring to bring in soil and plants. The families, teachers, and children all come together on Gardening Day to plant and work together to create a garden for each class. The children take care of the garden, and everyone can see the progress.

Watching changes in nature can happen all year long. For example, children can select a tree and chart how the leaves change or how the grass turns brown, or they can measure the snow that covers the ground or the rain that falls each day or each week. They can also notice what the garden looks like in each season. Children can chart the changes in notebooks, with pictures and charts. This tradition marks the seasons and also gives children an amazing nature-learning experience. Some families may even grow so inspired by the school garden that they start a garden with their children at home. Let families know about the Green Hour, a movement by the National Wildlife Federation in which families agree to have their children spend time in nature for one hour a day. Busy families might start with one hour a week.

Sporting events. For more than 20 years, one of Jacky's favorite summer traditions was celebrating the start of the WNBA basketball season and attending a game with the children she taught. Ms. Alina, a teacher whom Jacky has coached and who now is a fan of women's basketball, has adopted this tradition by attending games with the children she teaches. Many traditions begin with the things that teachers love and cherish. Teachers are often the constant in a class as each year some children and families leave and new ones join the class. Creating and maintaining traditions that teachers love fosters a sense of stability, place, and community.

Young adults who were once in Jacky's preschool class still talk about the Washington Mystics because that is the team Jacky and the children followed together. Some have even become season ticket holders with their families. Traditions started in classrooms can become traditions for families. See the article "Following Your Passion: Introducing Preschoolers to Basketball" (Howell 2013).

In-town tourists. For those programs that are year round, how can you create a tradition reflective of a different time of the year? One District of Columbia preschool program's tradition is called Seeing DC. Each summer they spend one week being tourists in their town. This tradition includes making "binoculars" for sightseeing and documenting the experience with an ongoing Seeing DC book that is shared every year with the class.

Consider the seasons of the year in your community and geographical area. How could the passing of seasons be recognized and celebrated at your early childhood setting? It can be something as simple as adopting a place outdoors and following its changes, watching tadpoles turn into frogs every spring, watching cacti bloom in April followed by prickly pears in early May and saguaros from mid-May to mid-June, or holding an annual class picnic each summer or a cozy winter tea party. Choose something that is important to you, the children you teach, and their families. Consider the languages and cultures of the families. Share your ideas with the children and their families. Work together to come up with ideas and establish traditions. Remember that traditions make a difference because they connect children to a place, a time, a person, or a group of people. They can help children feel that they are a part of something, something that lasts from year to year, and that they are part of a community. As one mother said, "I remember the ducks—it was a great experience. How many places hatch ducks and let children go through the whole experience? The whole beautiful process. I remember watching and watching the eggs and waiting for them to hatch, listening to the children's vocabulary to expand to include words like hatch, duck, duckling, incubate, temperature, and embryo. And when they finally did, it was the dinner conversation every night!"

Creating Yearly Traditions

Holiday Traditions

Holidays can be celebrated at early childhood settings, but only if doing so is important to the children, families, and teachers and to the program. Traditions are often linked with holidays that may be cultural, religious, or both. When families gather together and share a meal at Thanksgiving with the traditional turkey, the recipe for the stuffing may be the one that Grandma used to make, and the meal may not be complete without pumpkin pie to finish. Other families celebrate religious holidays that are meaningful to them. In Amy's Jewish community nursery school, they celebrate Sukkot every fall. Amy and her preschoolers build a sukkah in the outdoor space outside of their classroom. They share a meal in the sukkah and learn about the traditions that mark this religious festival.

> **What is a sukkah?**
>
> A sukkah is a structure built with any material that provides shelter and shade as part of observing the eight days of Sukkoh.

There is much debate and guidance about programs celebrating holidays in school. What are culturally sensitive, inclusive ways to recognize and celebrate holidays, taking into account the religious significance that may be attached to them? Many authors, such as Louise Derman-Sparks and Julie Olsen Edwards (2010), Julie Bisson (1997), Ann Pelo and Fran Davidson (2000), Janet Gonzalez-Mena (2014), and Stacey York (2003), have written about how to work with your community to find a way that is appropriate for your early childhood setting.

In *Anti-Bias Education for Young Children and Ourselves*, Louise Derman-Sparks and Julie Olsen Edwards (2010) remark, "Holiday activities can be an important part of anti-bias education. When grounded in anti-bias principles, holiday activities support children's cultural identity and enhance their family's feelings of belonging to a school community. Anti-bias holiday activities are also a tool for broadening children's awareness of our diverse world, adding to their enjoyment of its cultural diversity, and teaching them about people who make important social contributions across a range of civic and religious traditions" (p. 135).

Bisson writes, "The 'holiday question' is a big one among teachers who teach preschool on up to high school. . . . Today teachers are more aware of the vast diversity amongst the children and families they serve and many have become sensitive to individual needs and wishes of families. They want more than anything to be respectful of those values, beliefs, and wishes and do not want to offend families" (2014, 1).

Yet, these authors also discuss the challenges. Holidays are often celebrated in schools with a party or event, but if we truly want to embrace diversity and different cultures, holidays should be a teaching moment in which we explain what the holiday means to the culture that celebrates it. Many schools do not celebrate holidays unless they are part of the school's culture. However, holidays can offer meaningful teaching moments. Bisson's article (2014) offers questions about holiday traditions for teachers, administrators, and families to consider and discuss. Derman-Sparks and Edwards talk about developing a holiday policy and give concrete examples that can be used in any program (2010). Children should be given an opportunity to learn about different holidays in a meaningful, respectful manner, not simply as a one-time "event." This will strengthen your classroom

as children find deeper meaning and connection to the diverse holidays and cultures celebrated by the children and families in your program.

Because families at Kimberly's center have various religious traditions, the teachers invite all families to share their practices and preferences. Interested families sign up to visit the center and tell the children about their holiday traditions. They are also asked to write a description of their tradition on a note card, which is posted on the Family Tradition board for families, children, and teachers to read. This allows families to share what is important to them, forging a connection not only with the classroom community but also with the entire school community. As suggested earlier in the chapter, work with teachers and families to make decisions that are developmentally and culturally sensitive. Asking families to share their traditions with others is one way to incorporate what is important to each and every family.

❖　❖　❖　❖　❖　❖

Traditions, and the rituals embedded in them, are an important way to celebrate the changing of seasons, the passing of milestones, and the sharing of annual holidays. Children, families, and teachers all have unique ways of recognizing these changes, but classroom or program traditions provide opportunities for building community. This can happen when a class plants a garden, shares a holiday tradition, or recognizes how the seasons are changing with songs and calendars. Such experiences bring people together with events that celebrate important times. Annual and seasonal traditions connect staff, families, and children and are unique to each class or program. Every year, find a way to create or expand on the traditions that are part of your program.

In the Next Chapter

The final chapter describes a number of ways to make rituals and traditions part of your unique classroom calendar and how to share them with families.

Reflections

- How do the children's interests, languages, and cultures influence the traditions you create?

- What are you going to use as an inspiration for a new event that may grow into a tradition in your classroom or program?

- What is the current holiday policy in your program? Does it work for your community? Are there changes you could make that might make it more inclusive? Consider reading and discussing with teachers and administrators in your community additional, meaningful ways you could include holidays in your program.

5

Creating Your Own Rituals and Traditions

Three children were sitting in the comfy corner in Jacky's preschool classroom. Lined up on a bookshelf were more than 20 photo albums, one for each of the Dinosaur Classrooms. The children pulled out three big photo albums and sat down in the cushy chair to look at them. Jacky listened to their comments about the pictures. Ally remarked, "Look, they didn't hatch ducks, they hatched baby chicks!" Jeremiah hooted, "Look, at the castle! They painted theirs green!" Smiling, Vincent pointed to a picture and said, "There is my big sister; she was in the CATS play." They continued discussing and comparing the well-established traditions that are part of their class, the Dinosaur Classroom.

Pillars of Security

In "Pillars of Security: Making Child Care Centers Secure Places," Greenman (1990b), describes four important elements that make up the pillars: people, place, routine, and ritual. He also explains how rituals are valuable aspects of life events, such as weddings, funerals, birthdays, holidays, and rites of passage. He explains that rituals in early childhood programs can serve the same purpose for children. The preceding chapters provide examples and outline some of the ways rituals and traditions can benefit not only children but also families and teachers.

Creating a strong, connected school community is important for children, teachers, and families, and rituals and traditions help create those bonds. As discussed throughout this book, rituals are not just habits or routines; they are purposeful and intentional acts that foster connections. "Rituals are repeated patterns of meaningful acts. If you are mindful of your actions, you will see the ritual patterns. If you see the patterns, you may understand them. If you understand them, you may enrich them" (Fulghum 1995, vi). Rituals become meaningful when they are intentionally created to reflect the interests and needs of children and adults, building connections every time they are used. According to Atlas, "Rituals create islands of calm and predictability" (2005, xiv), allowing children, families, and teachers to

- **Express caring and love**
  Example Ritual or Tradition: Greet each child with a special handshake, hug, or high five.
  Effect: Children feel recognized as individuals and welcomed as a member of the community. This creates a safe, secure place for learning and growing.

- **Give rhythm to life**
  Example Ritual or Tradition: Schedule an open house where families share a Bio Box with the class and other families, or hold a growing up celebration at the end of the year to celebrate the children's growth that has occurred throughout the year.
  Effect: Rituals and traditions that mark milestones allow children, families, and teachers to recognize and celebrate important life moments and changes.

- **Ease transitions**
  Example Ritual or Tradition: Use a shy pet like Ruffy the Dragon. Ruffy is afraid of loud voices. He won't come out at circle time until all the children are quiet. At circle time, Ruffy waits patiently for the children to settle down.
  Effect: Teachers use a concrete tool (Ruffy the puppet) that grabs the children's attention. The puppet makes transitions enjoyable and go more smoothly!

- **Make everyday events special**
  Example Ritual or Tradition: Engage children in conversations at lunch by asking them a question and waiting for each child to answer.
  Effect: This makes mealtime special by giving each child time to be part of the conversation or listen to others. It helps children expand their social skills and develop a rich vocabulary in addition to building bonds based on what they learn about one another.

What Is a Bio Box?

A Bio Box is a collection of 5–10 items that reflects who a family is. For example, a family might bring in a miniature camping lantern because they love to camp, a small menorah that is a symbol of their faith, a set of play dolls and a dog that shows every member of their family, a passport because the family travels a great deal, and a favorite children's book that reflects their love of reading together. When families share the items in their Bio Box, it often brings together families who have similar interests. At the same time, teachers learn about the children's families. They can use this information to connect with families and to explore ways to include and involve families in the program.

- **Create and reinforce history**

  Example Ritual or Tradition: Ask each family to make a family quilt section that reflects their lives. Sew the quilt pieces together and hang the family quilt in the classroom. At Kimberly's center, each class makes a quilt that represents the families and their history. This has now become a tradition for her program.

  Effect: A quilt display not only reinforces the family's history but also allows them to share it with others in the center, expanding the family community.

- **Link generations**

  Example Ritual or Tradition: During the winter holidays, invite families to come in and share a family tradition (making holiday cookies, lighting a menorah, making gingerbread houses, singing songs together, or any other activity that has been part of a family ritual or tradition). For example, in December Sonia has a month-long celebration of grandparents that encourages extended family to visit the classroom.

  Effect: Families begin to count on classroom traditions and look forward to these opportunities to be engaged in the program.

- **Create warm memories**

  Example Ritual or Tradition: When Jacky interviewed families for her thesis, many people shared wonderful memories. More than 90 percent of the memories were connected to the intentional rituals and traditions that she developed. Whether it was recalling the time the slow cookers did not work for the I Love You Dinner or the book read at the Growing-Up Party, the rituals and traditions were what the children and their families remembered.

  Effect: One way we learn from and hold on to things from our experiences is if they are connected to a positive emotion. Creating rituals and traditions can reinforce those memories.

- **Share values**

  Example Ritual or Tradition: Create a ritual or tradition based on a value that is important to you and your program. In Miriam's class they have a ritual of filling the kindness jar. When a child notices an act of kindness, they put a button in the jar and say what they witnessed. Miriam writes all of the kind moments in a book. At the end of the week, they open the jar, pull out each button, and talk about what each button represents—all the kindness that occurred in their classroom.

  Effect: The ritual helps children recognize and celebrate acts of kindness, demonstrating the value of kindness.

There are many ways to create and embrace rituals and traditions in early childhood programs. Some you may already have in place. For example, you may have a special way you welcome children every day, a seasonal event that families look forward to, or annual traditions that have occurred over the years. Previous chapters have described different types of rituals and traditions:

- Daily
- Weekly
- Monthly
- Yearly/seasonal
- Holidays/special celebrations
- Milestones

You may use one type or many. Each provides opportunities to connect with children and families in a way that is unique to you, the children, and their families. Rituals and traditions are important for fostering a feeling of belonging, helping everyone remember people and times in the past, building a foundation of predictability and security, teaching important values and class identity, holding people together during challenging times, establishing a sense of place, and connecting children, families, and staff to one another. Everyday events can be special if you intentionally plan rituals and traditions that reflect the interests and needs of the children, their families, and the school community. Rituals also support families' languages and cultures by creating an environment where different cultures are recognized, appreciated, and celebrated. By singing welcoming songs in a home language, inviting families into the classroom to share their traditions, bringing in your own family rituals to the classroom, and creating a space that is loving and representative of your class, you can develop a place where children can learn and grow.

In *Learning Together With Young Children*, Curtis and Carter (2008) write, "The human family thrives on rituals and celebrations. . . . Rituals may be simple or elaborate and consciously or not, they are created with a longing to honor or create a memory, often employing symbolic gestures or objects. . . . The symbolic importance of a ritual may not be uncovered until they explore this memory later in their lives" (49). Memories of rituals and traditions live on. They make a difference!

Suggestions for Next Steps

It often takes mindfulness to a notice moment when you are connecting with someone, a moment that can be an important source for creating a meaningful and intentional ritual. Jasmine, a cooperative nursery school teacher, shared a story about how a song became a special classroom ritual. Below is the story of how "Edelweiss" became her classroom song.

I was listening to Jonathan dictate his story for his journal.

"Mommy read me two stories and then she sang 'Little Bird' and 'Edelweiss.'"

"'Edelweiss?'" I asked. "I love that song!" I sang it to him. "That one?"

"Yes! Mommy, me, and Paulie sing it every night. It's our special bedtime song."

"Would you like to share it with the class?" I asked, and received an enthusiastic nod.

Jonathan has taught me other songs that are near and dear to his heart. At gathering time later, he stood up and belted out the tune in his own unique way, with a few endearing mispronunciations.

I noticed that Jonathan's version differed slightly from my remembered version, which was tunneled deep in my heart since first seeing *The Sound of Music*.

As Jonathan sang the song to the class and we all sang it together a few times, the sound of their sweet voices brought tears to my eyes. I told the class that the song was special in Jonathan's family and that it was a favorite of mine too. The two co-op parents in the classroom clasped their hands over their hearts and held back tears as the children sang. After the children finished singing, they said that they loved the song too.

The next morning after we sang our usual morning circle song, Ricardo stood up and said, "I think Sylvie and Amanda (our co-op parents for the day) would like to hear how beautifully we sing 'Edelweiss.'" And so we sang it again. It was clear by the look on the faces of the co-op parents that they shared a similar passion for the song. They quietly whispered a heartfelt thanks to the children for sharing their rendition of the song.

Every day for two weeks we repeated this ritual, singing for each team of co-op parents until they'd all heard it. When we'd get to the "warm and bright" line, the adults, who had joined us in song, would stumble as they sang Jonathan's special version, with the mispronunciations! "This is Jonathan's family's special version," I would explain, and we would all continue singing. Music is often used as a way to bring people together. This classroom's choice arose spontaneously and was adopted by the children and me as a warm, special way to start the day. Each day the children would ask each day to sing it for whomever was there or just to sing together.

This ritual in Jasmine's class evolved naturally, which is sometimes the way rituals begin. Paying attention to what interests children will give you the information you need to develop a ritual or tradition and, as happened in Jasmine's class, following their lead may encourage their interests to grow into a classroom or program ritual.

What sayings, songs, and chants are meaningful to you that you repeat over and over? Which ones do the children join in with you? What do you want the children to remember? "Skinnamarink" became the song that the children sang at every I Love You Dinner. What will emerge as your traditions?

How to Begin Creating Rituals and Traditions

"We are what we repeatedly do." —Durant [1961] 2006, 98

A place to start creating rituals and traditions is to remember the rituals and traditions that were part of your childhood or are part of your life now, or to ask families to share their rituals and traditions. What is already important to you, the children, and their families? Is there a way to incorporate these ideas into the classroom? How can you develop or expand a ritual that already exists? Imber-Black, Roberts, and Whiting (2003) suggest choosing one ritual that has strong meaning to you and then visualize the experience. The ideas in the box "Reflections About Creating Rituals and Traditions" draw from information in "Using Rituals and Traditions to Create Classroom Community for Children, Teachers, and Parents" (Scully & Howell 2008).

Jacky remembers sitting on her grandmother's lap listening to stories. One story that her grandmother read to her every year was *My Father's Dragon*, by Ruth Stiles Gannett. Jacky has a photograph (see p. 111) where she is sitting on her grandmother's lap listening to a book. Each time Jacky visited her grandmother, they would read another chapter. This became a tradition, a special time for Jacky and her grandmother.

When Jacky became a preschool teacher, she continued the tradition of reading chapter books to the children she taught. One of the first books she read was *My Father's Dragon*. Children she taught still remember listening to the story of Elmer Elevator rescuing the baby dragon and following the adventures from the book. Each year the children experienced the book in

Reflections About Creating Rituals and Traditions

Reflecting on the following is one way to start determining what rituals and traditions mean to you so you can begin developing classroom rituals and traditions that are appropriate for the children and their families.

What do you remember about your childhood traditions and rituals? What makes these memories meaningful? In order to remember the moments in your life may relate to a tradition, consider the following:

• What celebrations were part of your childhood? What people, images, or aromas come to mind when recalling that celebration? How are your memories similar to and different from those of the children in the class? What can you learn from families who have different traditions?

• Take an imaginary "walk" around the neighborhood or area where you lived when you were a child. Describe what you would see, hear, and smell. Take the children on a walk around your community and see what they notice, hear, smell, and say.

• What songs do you remember from your childhood? Do you sing any of those songs now? What songs do the children sing and listen to? Are they similar? Bring in music to share with children and ask them to do the same. Note what is similar. What is different? Do you like both? Do they? Why or why not?

• Think about one of your favorite years in school. What do you remember about the teachers? The school environment or activities? Ask the children what they like about the classroom or the activities. What do they miss about school when they are home? Ask the children's families what their children say they like about school.

• Describe your childhood hiding place or special thinking place. Include as many details as possible. Ask the children where they like to hide. Have them show you or draw their favorite spots and tell you why it is the best place.

• Which grandparent or family member is or was special to you? Why is or was this person special to you? Bring in pictures of this family member and share the photos and stories of the person with your class. Ask them to bring in a picture of a family member who is special to them and share stories with the class.

• When you were a child, what toy or game did you like to play? Do you still have that toy or game? Do you play that game with your own children or children you teach? If you still have that toy or game, bring it in to share with the children or see if you can re-create it. What are the children's favorite toys at school and at home? Ask them what they like about the toys.

• What are the books that were read to you or stories that were told to you when you were a child? Share the stories with the children. Have them share a story with you. Then see what is similar about the stories. Why are these stories special to you?

Ideas inspired by Scully & Howell 2008.

their own way. One class decided Elmer needed a sister for the adventure (they named her Elisa), and they added her as Jacky read the book to them. What remained the same from year to year was the feeling of sitting cozily together and sharing the adventures of Elmer. This tradition continued until Jacky stopped teaching. Now she recommends developing a tradition of reading chapter books, including *My Father's Dragon*, to the teachers she coaches.

Remembering a meaningful ritual in your own life helps you identify the important pieces that go into creating rituals for the classroom. Chapter 2 outlines the three key elements of a ritual:

- Intentionality
- Tools and techniques
- Individualization

Intentionality

In *Ritual and Its Consequences* (Seligman et al. 2008), the authors state that ritual "involves the endless work of building, refining, and rebuilding webs of relationships in an otherwise fragmented world. The work of ritual ceaselessly builds a world that, for brief moments, creates pockets of order, pockets of joy, and pockets of inspiration" (180). The authors discuss how rituals support social interactions as well as build community.

Individuals have their own routines, as do early childhood settings. All programs have daily routines, transitions, and special events. You can use many of these to create new rituals and traditions. In *Everyday Traditions* (Atlas 2005), she quotes William J. Doherty, "You have to feed your children, so start with improving the quality of those feeding rituals. . . . You probably have birthday parties, holiday celebrations . . . explore the possibilities for enhancing those ordinary routines" (xii). In a similar fashion, look at the daily, weekly, or monthly events in the classroom or program and develop them into rituals.

Determine a need, then choose a routine or transition time to which you can add something extra that makes that time easier for children or that connects them to the classroom community. One difficult transition in many classrooms is when children go outdoors. What ritual can you develop that has a clear purpose with the secondary goal of connecting together as a community? In Andrea's pre-K class, she assigns buddies in the beginning of the week, changing the buddies each week to give children opportunities to work with each other. She makes the selection of buddies special by chanting the children's names as she assigns them. The buddies do many things together during the week, including looking for one another before heading outside and helping each other find what they need before going outside. Rituals provide an opportunity not only to connect but also to reinforce values. Andrea's class values friendship and caring, so she and the children created this ritual to strengthen that value. What is important to you, the children, their families, the program? Do your rituals reflect these values?

Rituals and traditions are also good practice. According to NAEYC's position statement on developmentally appropriate practice, teachers consider "what is known about the social and cultural contexts in which children live— referring to the values, expectations, and behavioral and linguistic conventions that shape children's lives at home and in their communities that practitioners must strive to understand in order to ensure that learning experiences in the program or school are meaningful, relevant, and respectful for each child and family" (NAEYC 2009a, 10). Children thrive and learn in a classroom environment that has rituals that respect and celebrate their individuality and in a school community that they feel part of because it reflects their interests. Classroom rituals help strengthen the bond between the school and home communities.

Thinking of everyday events or routines as something to celebrate is one way to begin focusing on rituals that reflect your uniqueness and the uniqueness of the children you teach. Rituals can help you and the children slow down and pay attention to the moment. Over time, rituals can grow into meaningful traditions that show that your classroom or program is a special learning place for children, families, and teachers.

Tools and Techniques

When you create rituals, you use tools and techniques that add meaning to the experience and that engage children and adults. Examples of the tools that are used in the rituals described in this book include music, sounds from instruments, chants, puppets, and other materials. The techniques include gestures and tone of voice. To decide which tools or techniques to include in a ritual, consider the following questions:

- What objects can you use to build connections between the people and the events of the ritual?
- How can you engage the senses?
- How can you incorporate music, poetry, or chants?
- What objects, like a puppet, could be part of the ritual?
- What visual, like a chart, could you create that would remind children of the steps that are part of a ritual?
- What elements from nature can you use?
- How can you incorporate movement or stories into the ritual?

- How can you include a living thing—a class pet, plants, or a garden—in your ritual?
- What classroom object can you use?
- Are there times of year that are significant for your program? Religious holidays? Beginning of the year? Season changes? Can you build rituals around these occasions?
- Have returning families told you what they remember most about the class, such as a song, an event, or a welcome? Think about taking something that is already significant and developing it into a ritual.

Individualization

One of the most important elements in creating your own unique rituals is to make them personal and meaningful to the children, their families, and if possible the staff. The I Love You Dinner was special in Jacky's classroom because it had personal meaning to those teachers, children, and families. In another program the menu, song, and invitation would be different. It would

Routine or Event	A one-time event or classroom or program routine.
Ritual	To make it a ritual, add intentionality, individuality, and a tool or technique that is meaningful to the children, their families, or the school community.
Tradition	Over time and with repetition, this ritual may become a tradition because the class or the program embraces its purpose. It then becomes ingrained in the life of the classroom or the program.
Purpose Intentionality	Define what you would like to accomplish with the ritual: For example, is it to connect people, ease the stress associated with a time of day, reinforce the values of the program, help children learn social skills, or develop a supportive classroom learning environment?
Personal Individualize	Personalize the ritual: For example, how does the ritual reflect the interests, needs, languages, and culture of the children you teach? If, for example, there are children in the class who are dual language learners, is part of the ritual in the language or languages of those children?
Tools Techniques	Use a tool or technique to add meaning to the ritual: For example, choose songs and dances that reflect the classroom personality, the languages or culture of the children, or the needs and interests of the children.

reflect the children, families, and teacher in that class. Having an I Love You Dinner may be something you choose to do, and involving the children and families in your class will make it meaningful.

How to Engage Families

Life is so busy that it is often hard for families and teachers to maintain important connections. Parents hurry in to drop off their children and rush at the end of the day at pickup time so they can beat traffic. It can be difficult to find the time to talk to families. How can you develop reciprocal relationships with them? Rituals and traditions can connect families, children, and teachers. These connections support the development of trusting, caring relationships and the creation of a wider family that incorporates children, families, and teachers.

Questions to Ask	What to Do Next	How to Continue
What is important to the children?	Do they love a specific story, book, or song? Consider expanding on what they connect to and enjoy. If they love a book, you might want to extend their interest by having the children act out the story of the book. Ask them to dress as the characters. Perform the story for the families who can attend the performance and tape it to share with the remaining families and so children can revisit the experience.	Involve children and families by asking them to share their ideas and stories or help make costumes or gather materials. Make programs for the play. Invite other classes to attend and have everyone share in the ritual with the class.
What is important to you (for example, animals, music, art, nature)?	Think about how you can bring something about your interests to the children you teach (for example, bring in some music, create a chant, get a class pet, organize a trip to an art gallery or a museum).	Grow this ritual by using it daily. Start with playing the music, then sing the song in circle time, act it out, make up class lyrics, perform it for the children's families. It is hard to predict where a ritual will go, but start with something that is meaningful to you and share it with the classroom community.
What are the moments when you need to connect with children or families? Are there times of the day when the class or individual children struggle? Would a ritual help?	Is drop-off time challenging for some children? Do certain children need a moment to connect to you? Consider an I Love You ritual. Play a welcome song when the children arrive each day. Set up a box of easy-to-reach comfort toys that children can play with at arrival time.	Invite families to contribute to the comfort toy box. Ask families of dual language learners to teach you a few key phrases in their home language. Ask their families about the songs their children love and play these songs at arrival time. Grow this welcoming ritual over time. Ask families to write down a family ritual or bring in a family photo or an object that is part of a family ritual (a song, book read every night, a candle lit each night that a parent is away, etc.).

(continued on next page)

What are values that the families in your class share? What are the values of individual families? Can you incorporate them in the classroom?	Is your class part of a religious program? Is your program eco-friendly? Do you value giving back to the community? Consider a ritual of giving back to your community, such as visiting a nursing home or creating cards for soldiers who are overseas.	Find out what is important to the children's families. Ask the families to suggest ways that the class and program can get involved. Are there military families at your program? What about families in need? How can you connect to the community? Invite the people from the surrounding community to the school for a give-back day or have the children go out into the community to get to know your area. For example, they can pick up trash in a park or visit the post office or local doctor's office. These are learning experiences for the children and opportunities for the community to meet and connect to the children and your program.
Who do you need to connect with most? A struggling child? A parent in crisis? A group of children?	What is your biggest struggle? How can a ritual help? For example, choose a parent or child you find challenging to connect with. Create a welcoming ritual with this parent or child. See if taking a few brief moments to connect helps you and them.	Expand the connecting rituals to coworkers, supervisors, and other people you need to work well with.

At Kimberly's center, the families of children who were preparing to go to kindergarten were asking her questions such as

- Who will welcome our child?
- Who will know our child?
- Who will hug our child when he or she is hurt?
- How will I feel a part of my child's school when I don't even walk my child into the classroom?
- Will I meet the teachers before school starts?
- How will I know what my child does all day?
- How will I know if there are any problems or concerns?

Kimberly noticed that families who were confident dropping off their children at her center were panicking about leaving the center and going into the unknown world of elementary school. They felt that their children were well prepared for kindergarten, but they were worried that as parents they were not prepared for the changes that lay ahead. To alleviate their fears and help families who had been a part of the school community for years, Kimberly created the Kindergarten Readiness Panel. She invited alumni families to return and share stories of their experiences in kindergarten, what they wish they had known, what might be a concern for families, and how to advocate for their children. What began as a one-time event to meet the needs of a few families has become an annual tradition. Alumni families bring report cards, artwork, lesson plans, memos, and materials to share with families of soon-to-be kindergartners. Families look forward to it all year and count on it to ease their transition into elementary school. It also allows current families and alumni families to connect and help each other.

Another tradition is that all departing families send a First Day of Kindergarten photo to Kimberly, who uses the photos to make a collage of graduates from each classroom. It connects the children and teachers who remain with those who have left. It also gives the new kindergartners the feeling that they are still connected to their preschool. When alumni children and families return to the center, they want to see the First Day of Kindergarten photos. The connections, the memories, and the sense of identity fostered by rituals and traditions remain with children and families long after they leave the classroom.

Consider other ways to engage families in the classroom and program community. Here are a few ideas:

- Ask families to volunteer. Some programs require families to volunteer, but all programs can ask families to shop for supplies, help in classrooms by reading to children, take care of school pets during vacations, assist with events such as birthday parties and field trips, and much more. What ritual can you establish that welcomes volunteers and recognizes their contribution to the classroom? One program organizes a Volunteer Thank-You Party each year to recognize the contributions that family members made that year.

- Ask family members, especially parents of dual language learners, to sign up to be a special reader and come in each week to read a book at circle time in English or their home language. You can schedule this at the beginning or end of the day so more family members can participate.

- Ask families to bring in fresh flowers each week. The families in each class sign up at the beginning of the year. On their chosen week, the child and his or her parent go to the store together to choose flowers that will go in his or her classroom, brightening it up and reminding the child of the moment spent picking out the special flowers.

- Host Gardening Day on a Saturday or school day depending on what works best at your center. Families can come in with their children and work with the staff to dig, weed, plant, and tend gardens. The children continue to care for the gardens, which were created by the community.

- Host special events like Trunk or Treating. Families and teachers decorate the trunks of their cars for Halloween and children go trick or treating from car to car. This allows families to spend time with one another and, for many, provides an opportunity to trick or treat safely.

- Create a slide show with videos and pictures of the children to use in parent–teacher conferences so families have an opportunity to see their child at work.

Involving families in rituals and traditions is an opportunity to enjoy and learn from every moment together. Part of involving families is listening to what they have to say about their children and what they wish and hope for their children. An open, respectful dialogue with families fosters connections so they feel that they are part of the school community. It allows connections to grow from child to child and from children and teachers to families and the wider community.

Conclusion

"Our participation in this rich range of rituals enables us to make meaning of our ever-changing lives. Rituals help us recognize who we are and what we value and to come together in community to share and acknowledge both the joy and pain of success."

—Imber-Black and Roberts 1992, 23

Another birthday goes by, the holiday season ends, a child graduates, a baby is born, and another cup of coffee in a special mug is shared with a loved one. These and many other similar events linger in our minds, make us feel joyful and peaceful, connect us to others in meaningful ways, and leave us with many memories. And when you look back on these times, most of them include rituals and traditions.

When Jacky interviewed families whose children she taught, they shared memories of rituals and traditions that were part of the classroom and the program. One of the dads who had two children attend the Dinosaur Classroom said to her, "You always said that once you were a Dinosaur, you are always a Dinosaur, and that was something bigger than you know. And in part, that happened because you were a constant, and then a community was built. Our family still carries on some of the traditions that happened when our children were in the Dinosaur preschool" (Howell 2007, 54). A mother said, "When my sons first went to kindergarten, it was a difficult adjustment for me, and I was constantly comparing everything to the way it was done in the Dinosaur Classroom. I finally got out of the habit of longing for the community sense we had with all the children and families. Beyond the parent/family community sense, was the classroom as a community. I remember the emphasis on the 'greater good'" (Howell 2007, 56). It was clear that the rituals and traditions established in the Dinosaur Classroom influenced the children and their families, an effect that lasted for years.

On a daily basis, the authors see positive results when teachers use rituals and traditions as one of the methods to build community and create a safe, caring environment where children are able to learn and develop. It makes a difference! In Kimberly's center, rituals are also a way of connecting the staff. On the first Wacky Day at Kimberly's center, she dressed up in a bizarre and hilarious outfit that made the children, staff, and families giggle and laugh. The next year, everyone waited to see what strange ensemble she would wear for Wacky Day. Many took photographs that were displayed outside each classroom and around the school. One parent made a sign called Week of the Young Director with a collage of Kimberly wearing silly outfits. Kimberly posted it in the hallway.

To encourage others to participate and dress up, Kimberly developed a contest for best ensemble. The winners' photographs were taken and posted in the hallway. The next year, the staff decided to dress up as wacky twins, every teacher in the center paired with another. Each pair came up with hilarious outfits, from characters from the game Operation to Hawaiian twins to a Victor/Victoria duo! A teacher who celebrates Wacky Day with enthusiasm each year says

that one of the reasons she commutes so long to her job and works as hard as she does is because of traditions like Wacky Days and the camaraderie resulting from staff rituals at the center. She says that fun staff rituals make her feel close to the school community. She would not trade this job for any other!

In one of the many memorable presentations by Bev Bos, she said, "Traditions don't have to be old, they need to be personal and peculiar and focus on what's important" (2013). Listen to the song "Memories" written by the late Tom Hunter and performed with Bev Bos and Michael Leeman. The song captures the essence of how the everyday moments celebrated by rituals and traditions are the truly important things in life.

❖   ❖   ❖   ❖   ❖   ❖

Rituals and traditions have always had a place in the home and in the family. We believe they also have an important role in early childhood programs and classrooms. Children, families, and teachers can benefit from the connections and sense of community that rituals and traditions can provide. In this environment, children can grow and learn, knowing that their learning and development will be supported by the adults in their lives. High-quality early childhood classrooms and programs include an environment where children and families feel safe and welcomed in a strong, caring, and connected community. Children, families, and teachers all benefit in an environment where they can learn about one another and share personal and unique moments and experiences each day, week, month, and year. Rituals and traditions provide an opportunity to connect in meaningful ways that children, families, and teachers may remember for years to come.

We have shared our stories and experiences of creating unique rituals and tradition. We hope that you begin using some of them or that you use them or the information in this book to develop the rituals and traditions that meet the needs, interests, languages, and cultures of the children you teach and their families. We wonder what memories you will be creating! May those memories last a lifetime and wrap their arms around you, the children, and the families!

References

Atlas, N. 2005. *Everyday Traditions: Simple Family Rituals for Connection and Comfort*. Poughkeepsie, NY: Amberwood Press.

Bailey, B. 1997. *I Love You Rituals: Activities to Build Bonds and Strengthen Relationships*. Oviedo, FL: Loving Guidance.

Bailey, B.A. 2000. *I Love You Rituals*. New York: HarperCollins.

Bailey, B. 2011. *Creating a School Family: Bully-Proofing Classrooms Through Emotional Intelligence*. Oviedo, FL: Loving Guidance.

Beneke, S.J., M.M. Ostrosky, & L.G. Katz. 2008. "Calendar Time for Young Children: Good Intentions Gone Awry." *Young Children* 63 (3): 12–16. www.naeyc.org/files/tyc/file/CalendarTime.pdf.

Bisson, J. 1997. *Celebrate! An Anti-Bias Guide to Enjoying Holidays in Early Childhood Programs*. St. Paul, MN: Redleaf Press.

Bisson, J. 2014. "Rethinking Holidays From an Anti-Bias Perspective." Accessed June 1. http://faculty.weber.edu/rwong/edu3200/Eng-RethinkingHolidays.pdf.

Biziou, B. 2000. *The Joy of Family Rituals: Recipes for Everyday Living*. New York: St. Martin's Press.

Bos, B. 2013. "Creative Art, Music, and Language." Workshop presented at the VAECE Annual Conference, Reston, VA, February.

Boyes, K. 2006. "Rituals Enrich Your Classroom." *Education Today* 6: 17.

Carson, R. 1965. *The Sense of Wonder*. New York: Harper & Row.

Carter, M. 2003. "Transitions, Rituals, and Celebrations." *Child Care Information Exchange* 152: 19–21.

Colker, L.J. 2005. *The Cooking Book: Fostering Young Children's Learning and Delight*. Washington, DC: NAEYC.

Colker, L.J., & F. Simon. 2014. "Cooking With STEAM." *Teaching Young Children* 8 (1): 10–13.

Conscious Discipline. 2014. "The School Family: The Foundation for Connections." Accessed April 25. http://consciousdiscipline.com/about/the_school_family.asp.

Corbey-Scullen, L., & J. Howell. 1997. "Out of the Housekeeping Corner and Onto the Stage: Extending Dramatic Play." *Young Children* 52 (6): 82–88.

Cox, M. 2003. *The Book of New Family Traditions: How to Create Great Rituals for Holidays and Everyday.* PA: Running Press.

Cox, M. 2012. *The Book of New Family Traditions: How to Create Great Rituals for Holidays and Every Day.* Expanded and updated ed. Philadelphia, PA: Running Press.

Crepeau, I.M., & M.A. Richards. 2003. *A Show of Hands: Using Puppets With Young Children.* St. Paul, MN: Redleaf Press.

Curtis, D. 2004. "Creating Invitations for Learning." *Child Care Information Exchange* 157: 38–40. http://childcareexchange.com/library/5015738.pdf.

Curtis, D., & M. Carter. 2008. *Learning Together With Young Children: A Curriculum Framework for Reflective Teachers.* St. Paul, MN: Redleaf Press.

Davis, J. 2001. "Caregivers' Corner. The Day Pork Chop Died (Almost)." *Young Children* 56 (3): 85.

Deal, T.E., & K.D. Peterson. 1999. *Shaping School Culture: The Heart of Leadership.* San Francisco, CA: Jossey-Bass.

Dengel, J. 2000. "Family Rituals and Traditions: Now More Important Than Ever." http://webshare.northseattle.edu/fam180/topics/traditionscelebs/Preschoolers%20Today%20Family%20Rituals%20and%20Traditions%20Now%20More%20Important%20Than%20Ever.htm.

Derman-Sparks, L., & J.O. Edwards. 2010. *Anti Bias Education for Young Children and Ourselves.* Washington, DC: NAEYC.

Doherty, W.J. 1999. *The Intentional Family: Simple Rituals to Strengthen Family Ties.* New York: Avon Books.

Durant, W. 1926. *The Story of Philosophy: The Lives and Opinions of the World's Greatest Philosophers From Plato to John Dewey.* New York: Pocket Books.

Fulghum, R. 1995. *From Beginning to End: The Rituals of Our Lives.* New York: Random House.

Galinsky, E. 2001. "The Balancing Act: Creating Everyday Rituals Your Kids Will Always Remember." *Leading Issues.* www.leadershipforwomen.com.au/images/Journal/Leading%20Issues%20Journal%20July%202001.pdf.

Gillespie, L., & S. Petersen. 2012. "Rituals and Routines: Supporting Infants and Toddlers and Their Families." Rocking and Rolling. *Young Children* 67 (4): 76–77.

Gonzalez-Mena, J. 2014. *50 Strategies for Communicating and Working With Diverse Families.* 3rd ed. Upper Saddle River, NJ: Pearson.

Greenman, J. 1988. *Caring Spaces, Learning Places: Children's Environments That Work.* Redmond, WA: Exchange Press.

Greenman, J. 1990a. "Pillars of Security." *Child Care Information Exchange* 71: 37–38.

Greenman, J. 1990b. "Pillars of Security: Making Child Care Centers Secure Places." *Child Care Information Exchange* 72: 18–19.

Greenman, J. 1998. *Places for Childhoods: Making Quality Happen in the Real World.* Redmond, WA: Exchange Press.

Greenman, J. 2005. *Caring Spaces, Learning Places: Children's Environments That Work*. Redmond, WA: Exchange Press.

Howell, J. 2007. "Rituals and Traditions in Early Childhood Classrooms: Tools for Building Classroom Community" (master's thesis, Pacific Oaks College).

Howell, J. 2013. "Following Your Passion: Introducing Preschoolers to Basketball." *Teaching Young Children* 6 (4): 10–13. www.naeyc.org/tyc/article/following-your-passions.

Hyson, M. 2008. *Enthusiastic and Engaged Learners: Approaches to Learning in the Early Childhood Classroom*. New York: Teachers College Press; Washington, DC: NAEYC.

Imber-Black, E., & J. Roberts. 1992. *Rituals for Our Times: Celebrating, Healing, and Changing Our Lives and Our Relationships*. New York: HarperCollins.

Imber-Black, E., J. Roberts, & R.A. Whiting, eds. 2003. *Rituals in Families and Family Therapy*. Rev. ed. New York: W.W. Norton & Company.

Isbell, R. 2015. "An Environment That Positively Impacts Young Children." *Earlychildhood NEWS*. Accessed March 31. www.earlychildhoodnews.com/earlychildhood/article_view.aspx?ArticleID=334.

Jensen, E. 2009. *Super Teaching: Over 1000 Practical Strategies*. 4th ed. Thousand Oaks, CA: Corwin Press.

Keen, S. 1994. *Hymns to an Unknown God: Awakening the Spirit in Everyday Life*. New York: Bantam Books.

Kersey, K.C., & M.L. Masterson. 2013. *101 Principles for Positive Guidance With Young Children: Creating Responsive Teachers*. Upper Saddle River, NJ: Pearson.

Levine, D.A. 2003. *Building Classroom Communities: Strategies for Developing a Culture of Caring*. Bloomington, IN: Solution Tree Press.

Maloney, C. 2000. "The Role of Ritual in Preschool Settings." *Early Childhood Education Journal* 27 (3) 143–50.

Manfredi/Petitt, L.A. 2014. "Building a Community Through Breakfast Club." *Teaching Young Children* 7 (3): 20–21. www.naeyc.org/tyc/files/tyc/breakfast.pdf.

Morrison, F.J. 2007. "Contemporary Perspectives on Children's Engagement in Learning." Symposium presented at the biennial meeting of the Society for Research in Child Development, Boston, MA.

NAEYC. 2009a. "Developmentally Appropriate Practice in Early Childhood Programs Serving Children From Birth Through Age 8." Position statement. Washington, DC: NAEYC. www.naeyc.org/positionstatements/dap.

NAEYC. 2009b. "When Someone Dies." Teachers' Lounge. *Teaching Young Children* 2 (5): 30.

Neugebauer, B. 2000. "Creating Community, Generating Hope, Connecting Future and Past: The Role of Rituals in Our Lives." *Child Care Information Exchange* 136: 48–51.

Pelo, A. & F. Davidson. 2000. *That's Not Fair! A Teacher's Guide to Activism With Young Children*. St. Paul, MN: Redleaf Press.

Rand, M.K. 2012. "Are You Harnessing the Power of Rituals in Your Classroom?" *The Positive Classroom* (blog), November 29. http://thepositiveclassroom.org/are-you-harnessing-the-power-of-rituals-in-your-classroom/.

Reinhard, K. 2014/2015. "Ten Ways to Teach Children About the World Without Leaving School." *Teaching Young Children* 8 (2): 7. www.naeyc.org/tyc/article/teach-about-the-world-without-leaving-school.

Roeser, R. 2014. "Social & Emotional Learning Through Kindness in the Classroom." Random Acts of Kindness Foundation. www.kaltura.com/index.php/extwidget/preview/partner_id/608752/uiconf_id/22595982/entry_id/0_27d6h1az/embed/iframe?

Scully, P., & J. Howell. 2008. "Using Rituals and Traditions to Create Classroom Community for Children, Teachers, and Parents." *Early Childhood Education* 36 (3): 261–66.

Scully, P., J. Howell, & L. Corbey-Scullen. 2000. "From a Bean Cake to a Classroom Kingdom: An Idea Becomes Five Weeks of Learning." *Young Children* 55 (3): 28–35.

Seligman, A.B., R.P. Weller, M.J Puett, & B. Simon. 2008. *Ritual and Its Consequences: An Essay on the Limits of Sincerity.* New York: Oxford University Press.

Smith-Bonahue, T., S. Smith-Adcock, & J.H. Ehrentraut. 2015. "'I Won't Be Your Friend If You Don't!' Preventing Relational Aggression in Preschool Classrooms." *Young Children* 70 (1): 76–83.

Spagnola, M., & B.H. Fiese. 2007. "Family Routines and Rituals: A Context for Development in the Lives of Young Children." *Infants & Young Children* 20 (4): 284–99.

Stewart, D.J. 2013. "Tips for Building a Sense of Community in the Preschool Classroom." *Teach Preschool* (blog), September 6. www.teachpreschool.org/2013/09/tips-for-building-a-sense-of-community-in-the-preschool-classroom.

Taharally, C., & E. La Fontaine. 2007. "Developmentally Appropriate Practice and Preschool Graduation." *Young Children* 62 (3): 72–75.

Webber, L. 2011. "Marking Time: The Significance of Anniversaries." *Psychology, Philosophy & Real Life* (blog), September 7. http://counsellingresource.com/features/2011/09/07/marking-time-anniversaries/.

Wright, T. 2014. "Too Scared to Learn: Teaching Young Children Who Have Experienced Trauma." Research in Review. *Young Children* 69 (5): 88–93.

York, S. 2003. *Roots and Wings: Affirming Culture in Early Childhood Programs.* Rev. ed. St. Paul, MN: Redleaf Press.

Resources

Books

Alperson, M. 2001. *Dim Sum, Bagels and Grits: A Sourcebook for Multicultural Families*. New York: Farrar, Straus and Giroux.

Beck, R., & S.B. Metrick. 2003. *The Art of Ritual: Creating and Performing Ceremonies for Growth and Change*. Berkley, CA: Celestial Arts.

Biziou, B. 1999. *The Joys of Everyday Rituals: Spiritual Recipes to Celebrate Milestones, Ease Transitions, and Make Every Day Sacred*. New York: St. Martin's Press.

Bos, B. 1990. *Together We're Better: Establishing a Coactive Learning Environment*. Roseville, CA: Turn-the-Page-Press.

Bos, B. & J. Chapman. 2005. *Tumbling Over the Edge: A Rant for Children's Play*. Roseville, CA: Turn-the-Page-Press.

Chenfeld, M.B. 2014. *Still Teaching in the Key of Life: Joyful Stories From Early Childhood Settings*. Washington, DC: NAEYC; St. Paul, MN: Redleaf Press.

Chicola, N.A. & E.B. English. 2002. *Creating Caring Communities With Books Kids Love*. Golden, CO: Fulcrum Publishing.

Christopher, D. 1999. *Come to the Table: A Celebration of Family Life*. New York: Warner Books.

Cox, M. 1998. *The Heart of a Family: Searching America for New Traditions That Fulfill Us*. New York: Random House.

Curtis, D., & M. Carter. 2011. *Reflecting Children's Lives: A Handbook for Planning Your Child-Centered Curriculum*. 2nd ed. St. Paul, MN: Redleaf Press.

Davis, D. 1993. *Telling Your Own Stories: For Family and Classroom Storytelling, Public Speaking, and Personal Journaling*. Little Rock, AR: August House.

DeVinck, C. 1991. *Only the Heart Knows How to Find Them: Precious Memories for a Faithless Time*. New York: Viking Adult.

Doherty, W.J. 1997. *The Intentional Family: How to Build Family Ties in Our Modern World*. Reading, MA: Addison-Wesley.

Dresser, N. 1999. *Multicultural Celebrations: Today's Rules of Etiquette for Life's Special Occasions*. New York: Three Rivers Press.

Esche, M.B., & C.B. Braham. 1998. *Kids Celebrate! Activities for Special Days Throughout the Year*. Chicago, IL: Chicago Review Press.

Ferrucci, P. 2001. *What Our Children Teach Us: Lessons in Joy, Love, and Awareness.* New York: Warner.

Fitzjohn, S., M. Weston, & J. Large. 1993. *Festivals Together: Guide to Multicultural Celebration.* Stroud, Gloucestershire, UK: Hawthorn Press.

Freeman, J., & C.F. Bauer. 2015. *The Handbook for Storytellers.* Chicago, IL: ALA Editions.

Gillespie, P. 1997. *Of Many Colors: Portraits of Multiracial Families.* Amherst, MA: University of Massachusetts Press.

Lee, E., D. Menkart, & M. Okazawa-Rey, eds. 2002. *Beyond Heroes and Holidays: A Practical Guide to K-12 Anti-Racist, Multiclutural Education and Staff Development.* 2nd ed. Washington, DC: Teaching for Change.

Mardell, B. 1999. *From Basketball to the Beatles: In Search of Compelling Early Childhood Curriculum.* Portsmouth, NH: Heinneman.

Matthews, J., & C. Matthews. 1998. *The Winter Solstice: The Sacred Traditions of Christmas.* Wheaton, IL: Quest Books.

McGraw-Hill. 2009. *The Teacher's Calendar: The Day-by-Day Almanac of Historic Events, Holidays, Famous Birthdays, and More!, 2009-2010.* New York: McGraw-Hill.

McGraw-Hill. 2015. *Chase's Calendar of Events 2015.* New York: McGraw-Hill.

Menard, V. 2004. *The Latino Holiday Book: From Cinco de Mayo to Dia de los Muertos—The Celebrations and Traditions of Hispanic-Americans.* New York: Marlowe & Company.

Pals, F. M. 1996. *Create a Celebration: Ideas and Resources for Theme Parties, Holidays, and Special Occasions.* Golden, CO: Fulcrum Publishing.

Rogers, F. 2000. *The Giving Box: Create a Tradition of Giving With Your Children.* Philadelphia, PA: Running Press.

Sapon-Shevin, M. 2010. *Because We Can Change the World: A Practical Guide to Building Cooperative, Inclusive Classroom Communities.* 2nd ed. Thousand Oaks, CA: Corwin Press.

Teaching Tolerance Project. 1997. *Starting Small: Teaching Tolerance in Preschool and the Early Grades.* Montgomery, AL: Southern Poverty Law Center.

Tuleja, T. 1987. *Curious Customs: The Stories Behind 296 Popular American Rituals.* New York: Harmony Books.

Online Articles

Berke, K. 2012. "Before, After, Later, and Next: Using a Calendar in a Preschool Classroom." *Ideas and Inspiration for Early Childhood* (blog), August 14. www2. teachingstrategies.com/blog/44-before-after-later-and-next-using-a-calendar-in-a-preschool-classroom.

Church, E.B. 2014. "Building Community in the Classroom." Accessed June 1. *Early Childhood Today.* www.scholastic.com/teachers/article/building-community-classroom.

Greenberg, P. 2015. "The Value of Classroom Rituals & Routines." Accessed January 6. *Early Childhood Today.* www.scholastic.com/teachers/article/value-classroom-rituals-routines.

Greenman, J. 2005. "Places for Childhood in the 21st Century: A Conceptual Framework." *Young Children* 60 (3). www.naeyc.org/files/yc/file/200505/01Greenman.pdf

McKay, B., & K. McKay. 2013. "Creating a Positive Family Culture: The Importance of Establishing Family Traditions. *The Art of Manliness* (blog), October 9. www.artofmanliness.com/2013/10/09/creating-a-positive-family-culture-the-importance-of-establishing-family-traditions/.

Wilson, M B. 2011. "Mudge." *Responsive* (blog), July 1. www.responsiveclassroom.org/blog/mudge.

Music

"Everyone Needs to Rest," Jack Hartmann

I Love You Rituals CD, Becky Bailey and Mar Harman

Memories CD, Bev Bos, Michael Leeman and Tom Hunter

My Little World CD, Natii Wright

Staying Cool at School CD, Billy Brennan

Still the Same Me CD, Sweet Honey in the Rock

Children's Books

Allie's Basketball Dream (1996), by Barbara E. Barber. Illus. by Darryl Ligasan.

Anton Can Do Magic (2011), by Ole Konnecke.

Basketball Belles: How Two Teams and One Scrappy Player Put Women's Hoops on the Map (2011), by Sue Macy. Illus. by Matt Collins.

Cherry Pies and Lullabies (1998), by Lynn Reiser.

Children Just Like Me: Celebrations! (1997), by Barnabas and Anabel Kindersley

Days to Celebrate: A Full Year of Poetry, People, Holidays, History Fascinating Facts, and More (2005), by Lee Bennett Hopkins. Illus. by Stephen Alcorn.

Doctor Knickerbocker and Other Rhymes (1993), David Booth and Marilyn Kovalski.

Families (2000), by Ann Morris.

Go, Dog. Go! (1961), by P.D. Eastman.

Goodnight Moon (1947), by Margaret Wise Brown. Illus. by Clement Hurd.

Gorf's Pond (1996), by Fiona Hurlock. Illus. by Eric Kincaid.

The Hello, Goodbye Window (2005), by Norton Juster. Illus. by Chris Raschka.

The High Rise Glorious Skittle Skat Roarius Sky Pie Angel Food Cake (1990), by Nancy Willard. Illus. by Richard Jesse Watson.

I Am America (2003), by Charles. R. Smith.

The Kissing Hand (2006), by Aubrey Penn. Illus. by Ruth E. Harper and Nancy M. Leak.

Miss Tizzy (1993), by Libba Moore Gray. Illus, by Jada Rowland.

My Father's Dragon (1948), by Ruth Stiles Gannett. Illus. by Ruth Chrisman Gannett.

On the Day You Were Born (2012), by Debra Frasier.

One Smile (2002), by Cindy McKinley. Illus. by Mary Gregg Byrne.

Our Granny (1993), by Margaret Wild. Illus. by Julie Vivas.

Our People (2002), by Angela Shelf Medearis. Illus. by Michael Bryant.

Owl Babies (1992), by Martin Waddell. Illus. by Patrick Benson.

Roxaboxen (1991), by Alice McLerran. Illus. by Barbara Cooney.

Tell Me a Story, Mama (1989), by Angela Johnson. Illus. by David Soman.

Throw Your Tooth on the Roof: Tooth Traditions From Around the World (1998), by Selby B. Beeler. Illus. by G. Brian Karas.

Welcoming Babies (1994), by Margy Burns Knight. Illus. by Anne Sibley O'Brien.

What You Know First (1995), by Patricia MacLachlan. Illus. by Barry Moser.

When I Was Little: A Four-Year-Old's Memoir of Her Youth (1993), by Jamie Lee Curtis. Illus. by Laura Cornell.

Wish: Wishing Traditions Around the World (2008), by Roseanne Thong. Illus. by Elisa Kleven.

Organizations and Websites

Asia for Kids

www.asiaforkids.com

Despite the name of the organization, you can find books, videos, and materials that reflect many different cultural areas and span many areas of the world, including Africa and Latin America.

Bizarre, Wacky, and Unique Holidays

www.holidayinsights.com/moreholidays/

A resource for a variety of holidays and events to use as special days.

Center for Building a Culture of Empathy

http://cultureofempathy.com/

The Center for Building a Culture of Empathy offers resources and information about the values of empathy and compassion.

Childwork/Childsplay

www.childswork.com

The company's products target a range of social and emotional needs of children and adolescents and can be used by therapists, educators, and parents.

China Books and Periodicals

www.chinabooks.com

This is a wonderful source of books and merchandise about and from China.

Days of the Year

www.daysoftheyear.com/

Daily weird, funny, wonderful, and bizarre holidays.

Donnelly/Colt Progressive Resources

www.donnellycolt.com

A mail order business that has been designing and distributing progressive materials promoting peace, social and environmental justice, and human rights since 1975.

Foundation for a Better Life

www.values.com

The Foundation for a Better Life offers free resources for schools.

Holiday Insights

www.holidayinsights.com/everyday.htm

Major yearly holidays.

Holidays and Other Fun

www.brownielocks.com/

Great resource for a variety of bizarre, crazy, silly, unknown holidays, and observances.

Just Us Books
www.justusbooksonlinestore.com

Offers high-quality books on black heroes and African history, as well as the Afro-Bets series of books, targeting children ages 2–12.

Lectorum
www.lectorum.com

Lectorum offers the most comprehensive catalog of Spanish-language books for pre-K through eighth grade. These include translations of English language classics.

Lee & Low Books
www.leeandlow.com

A great resource for multicultural and multiethnic children's books, including some that focus on civil rights, women, single parents, and coping with death.

Live and Learn
www.liveandlearn.com

This interesting website offers an array of parenting materials as well as online activities for children.

Multicultural Kids
www.multiculturalkids.com

Provide high-quality multicultural materials for preschool and elementary school-age children. Their fun, informative, and diverse materials can be used to foster tolerance and an appreciation of differences.

Pan Asian Publications
www.panap.com

This is a terrific online store offering books in various Asian languages, in English translation, and in bilingual versions. The company has added publications in Spanish and Russian.

The Random Acts of Kindness Foundation
www.randomactsofkindness.org

Great resources for teachers that encourage acts of kindness.

Rethinking Schools
www.rethinkingschools.org

Rethinking Schools is a provocative journal for educators in the multicultural arena.

Syracuse Cultural Workers
Tools for Change
http://syracuseculturalworkers.com/

Resources of poster, buttons, books, and more that promote diversity.

Teaching for Change

www.teachingforchange.org

Teaching for Change provides teachers and parents with the tools to create schools where students learn to read, write, and change the world.

Teaching Tolerance

www.splcenter.org/what-we-do/teaching-tolerance

Teaching Tolerance is the name of a media education program sponsored by the Southern Poverty Law Center to counter bigotry and hater crimes and promote tolerance across races, religions, and ethnicities. The program offers free materials to educators.

About the Authors

Jacky Howell, MA, has worked in the field of early childhood education for more than 40 years. She worked at the Kensington/Forest Glen Children's Center as a teacher and assistant director and at Montgomery Child Care Association's Training Institute teaching courses, giving workshops, and keynoting for many years. She currently works as a consultant and trainer for early childhood programs in the Washington Metropolitan area and as a speaker and presenter internationally.

Jacky has authored articles in both *Young Children* and *Teaching Young Children* as well as other early childhood journals. For more than 25 years, Jacky has given keynotes and presentations at NAEYC conferences and at international conferences.

Jacky's knowledge of the power of rituals and traditions began when she was a child. Every time she visited her grandmother, Jacky would sit on her lap and listen to her grandmother read chapter books, an experience she still remembers.

Kimberly Reinhard, MSc, has been a director of Langley Children's Center serving infants to preschool children since 2008. She has also been a teacher in a toddler classroom, an afterschool teacher for kindergartners, a tutor for children of all ages, and a volunteer for children who live in a housing project in Washington, DC, and for children living in a home in St. Louis, Missouri, for children affected by HIV and drug addiction.

Kimberly speaks about rituals and traditions at NAEYC conferences and state conferences, and she has written for *Teaching Young Children* magazine. She is the chair of the Week of the Young Child committee for the Northern Virginia Association for Early Childhood Education and president of Friends of the Arlington Library.

In Kimberly's family, an important tradition was Sunday family dinner and a movie. They would make dinner and pick a movie to watch, have dinner on trays, simply enjoying being together. To this day, every time Kimberly goes home to visit her family, they always have dinner and a movie together.

Acknowledgments

We are both grateful to and appreciative of our colleagues, friends, and families who supported us through the ups and downs of writing this book. We are fortunate to be surrounded by so many amazing children, teachers, family members, and colleagues in the early childhood community.

This book, inspired by Jacky's master thesis, has been a long time coming. Once again, so many families and children from Kensington/Forest Glen Children's Center (KFGCC) provided additional stories and photos. Her time at KFGCC and the many amazing teachers she worked with were a valuable source for the examples in this book. Jacky feels very fortunate for all the learning opportunities and the special children and adults she worked with those many years at KFGCC. In addition, her work and supportive training colleagues at Montgomery Child Care Association's Training Institute gave her the opportunity to take what she learned and develop workshops to share ideas with other teachers around using rituals and traditions in the classroom. Kimberly was inspired by her time and work as both a teacher in early childhood programs and as the director of Langley Children's Center. Her interactions with children provided humorous and heartfelt reminders of the importance of the work she does in early childhood education.

Many of the examples and stories in this book are based on rituals and traditions used by teachers who Jacky and Kimberly have worked with. A special thank-you to schools in Washington, DC, and Virginia such as Langley Children's Center, CentroNía at Harvard Street, School for Friends, National Children's Center, and Martha's Table, especially to Beth Ann Moore at CentroNía for providing photographs.

We could not have written this book without the ideas, extra set of eyes, and support of colleagues. Special thanks goes to Pat Scully, who co-wrote an article on this topic with Jacky, Natalie Eades from CentroNía, and Paige Beatty from the House of Representatives Child Care Center.

At NAEYC we have been fortunate to work under the wise guidance of Kathy Charner, Liz Wegner, and Derry Koralek. We are grateful for your careful editing and support!

There are many who have inspired us as early childhood professionals. We want to mention the names of a few who affected, moved, and taught us—Bev Bos, Michael Leeman, Becky Bailey, the late Tom Hunter, Margie Carter, and Deb Curtis.

And of course, we could not have kept moving forward with this work if not for those special people in our lives. Kimberly is grateful for her supportive family, her generous friends, and amazing loved ones, without whom none of this would be possible. Jacky feels fortunate to have grown up in a family with traditions that her sister Susan continues to this day! Friends and family were a steady source of caring, love, and extra energy for both of us, especially as Jacky spent time at the women's basketball Final Four working on this book and as Kimberly finished up the book while working long hours at her center, chairing the Week of the Young Child committee for the Northern Virginia AEYC, and trying to find time to sleep! The time has finally come, and we are delighted to share this book with you!

Index